THE ROLE OF FATHER-LIKE CARE
IN THE EDUCATION
OF YOUNG BLACK MALES

THE ROLE OF FATHER-LIKE CARE IN THE EDUCATION OF YOUNG BLACK MALES

Aaron Lamont Horn

With a Foreword by
Susan Roberta Katz

The Edwin Mellen Press
Lewiston•Queenston•Lampeter

Library of Congress Cataloging-in-Publication Data

Horn, Aaron Lamont.
 The role of father-like care in the education of young black males / Aaron Lamont
Horn ; with a foreword by Susan Roberta Katz.
  p. cm.
 Includes bibliographical references and index.
 ISBN-13: 978-0-7734-3771-5
 ISBN-10: 0-7734-3771-1
 1. African American men--Education. 2. African American youth--Education. 3.
Tutors and tutoring--United States. I. Title.
 LC2731.H67 2010
 371.821--dc22

                          2010001533

hors série.

A CIP catalog record for this book is available from the British Library.

Front cover: This is a photograph of Mr. Calvin Thomas and his son. Mr. Thomas is a Civil
Service employee for the city and county of San Francisco, California. Mr. Thomas enjoys
reading and counseling at-risk youth in San Francisco.

            The Edwin Mellen Press   The Edwin Mellen Press
                 Box 450   Box 67
            Lewiston, New York   Queenston, Ontario
            USA 14092-0450   CANADA L0S 1L0

                     The Edwin Mellen Press, Ltd.
                     Lampeter, Ceredigion, Wales
                     UNITED KINGDOM SA48 8LT

               Printed in the United States of America

DEDICATION

For your unyielding dedication and support, I would like to dedicate this book to mom, Marc, and Soma. Thank you mom and Marc for always loving me completely. Soma, thank you for demonstrating the true meaning of a caring relationship. Our love for each other has enhanced my development as a human being.

TABLE OF CONTENTS

CHAPTER IV. PROFILES

CHAPTER V. FINDINGS

CHAPTER VI. DISCUSSION, RECOMMENDATIONS, AND CONCLUSION

APPENDIXES

LIST OF ILLUSTRATIONS

TABLES

FOREWORD

As Professor and Chair of International and Multicultural Education at the University of San Francisco, I am deeply honored to offer my words of highest praise for this book by Dr. Aaron L. Horn. In guiding the doctoral research of many talented and committed young educators, I speak of the need for them to write what I call "impassioned scholarship" – to open up their hearts to the people they are studying and to broaden their minds through a sophisticated analysis of the literature on their topics. I want to read their work and hear not only their own voices, but also the voices of their research participants and the theorists and scholars they have so diligently reviewed.

Dr. Horn's book truly embodies "impassioned scholarship." Through his dialogues with the young African American males whom he tutors in their homes, we learn about and live through the joys and sorrows in their experiences with education. Following Dr. Horn's example, we grow to care deeply about these boys and we gain the utmost respect for their resiliency to overcome many obstacles to their success. From the vivid portraits lovingly painted by Dr. Horn, we become familiar with Dario's critical thinking ability amidst external factors impeding his concentration at home, Jamie's insatiable curiosity and humor while dealing for many years with tragic loss, and Jerele's fierce motivation to attain good grades in the face of developmental damage from his mother's crack cocaine addiction. We learn of Jeremiah's passion for African American literature despite dealing with violence throughout his young life, Shareek's drive to study art in college notwithstanding his struggle with reading, Shane's skill at debating in contrast to his disinterest in school assignments, and Taylor's thrill at discovering African American history during tutoring sessions while remaining unchallenged by teachers at school.

Most clearly of all, we come to know Dr. Horn as an unusually dedicated teacher and loving father figure. Like his tutees, he was raised by single women in the same low-income, African American neighborhood and as a young boy, acted out in school and was labeled as a troublemaker. With tremendous self-discipline and sharply honed organizational skills, he became a brilliant scholar once he discovered his own passion for education. Thus he serves as a powerful role model for his youth on how to maintain a strong identity as a successful African American male.

Additionally, Dr. Horn's impassioned scholarship reveals itself in the way he brings to life Vygotsky's concept of the Zone of Proximal Development, Coleman's notion of social capital, and Ladson-Billings' and Tate's exposition of Critical Race Theory in education. These three theoretical perspectives are intertwined in an authentic way, deepening our understanding of the lived experiences of young African American males. Dr. Horn illustrates how a caring tutoring relationship can activate the expert-novice dynamic which Vygotsky identified as central to learning and which Coleman noted as critical for social networking.

Moreover, Dr. Horn delineates how Critical Race Theory provides an explanation for how and why African American males have historically and continually experienced inadequate education by uncovering the structural and institutional racism that run deep in this nation. At school, his students have endured constant discrimination from teachers who yell at them, act afraid of them, suspend them, mistreat them, and expect little of them – all because of their being Black males. The stories of Dr. Horn's tutees bring to life the words of W.E.B. Du Bois – the original Critical Race Theorist - written more than a century ago:

> So here we stand among thoughts of human unity, even through conquest and slavery; the inferiority of black men, even if forced by fraud; a shriek in the night for the freedom of men who themselves are not yet sure of their right to demand it. This is the tangle of thought and afterthought

wherein we are called to solve the problem of training men for life (W.E.B. Du Bois, 1903, p. 89).

The voices of critical theorists, and the researchers who have applied these views, resound loud and clear in this book.

After reading the participants' educational experiences and seeing the oftentimes-stark contrast between public school and in-home tutoring, it would be easy to conclude that tutoring has much greater value. However, Dr. Horn carefully avoids placing in-home, one-on-one tutoring in contention with public schooling. The carefully constructed research questions allow for an impartial dialogue to evolve among the research participants. As a result, the tutees do occasionally convey positive experiences with both public school and in-home, one-on-one tutoring. If educators reading this book pay attention to and build upon these experiences, they could dramatically improve their practice with African American male students.

In his conclusion, Dr. Aaron Horn identifies "father-like care" as being the element most central to the effectiveness of his in-home, one-on-one tutoring. This term captures several paternal aspects of his practice: being consistent and following through, holding high academic expectations, and inspiring others to succeed. "Father-like care" represents Dr. Horn's significant contribution, not only to the research literature on caring and the education of African American males, but also to his youth and the educators who serve them. In fact, this book is a gift to future teacher educators on how to practice authentic care among young African American males in education. I am genuinely proud to have served as Dr. Horn's advisor and to be the author of this foreword.

Dr. Susan Roberta Katz

Dr. Susan Roberta Katz is Professor at the University of San Francisco School of Education. She is also the current Chair of the Department of International and Multicultural Education and founder of the Human Rights Education emphasis in the department's MA and doctoral programs. This emphasis is the first of its kind in the U.S.

ACKNOWLEDGMENTS

I first would like to thank my Grandparents Cora and Archie Reynolds for your inspiration. To all of my aunts, uncles, cousins, and other extended family members from the Chriss, Gillette, Horn, Jackson, Mayo, Moore, Parish, Reynolds, Stepney, Threadgill, and Timmons family. Thank you for your encouragement. To my surrogate families: the Steeno's, the Salomon's, the Sen's, the Stewart's, the Collins family, Mr. Paul Mendez, Mr. Bobby Farlice, Dr. Suzan Katz, Dr. Onllwyn Dixon, Dr. Betty Taylor, Dr. Rosita Galang, Dr. Koirala-Azad, Dr. Emma Fuentes, Dr. Farbod Karimi, Mrs. Andrea McEvoy-Spero and family, Dr. Nabila Massoumi, Ms. Mi'jan Tho-Biaz Wilder and family, Mr. Brad Washington, Mr. Ken Yoshioka, Dr. Lois Moore, and Dr. Ben Baab. I thank all of you for your motivation, counseling, and wisdom.

To my USF Gleeson library staff: Dr. Tyrone Cannon, Mr. Joe Garity, Mr. Ross Psyhogios, Ms. Colette Hayes, Ms. Fabiola Hernandez, Ms. Sherise Kimura, Mr. Lloyd Affholter, Ms. Janine Gericke, Mr. Patrick Dunagan, Mr. Matthew Collins, Mr. Shawn Calhoun, and others. Thank you for your insight, mentorship, and high standard of professionalism. To my friends and community: Ms. Karen O'Grady, Mr. Dave Scott, Mr. Robert Lucas, Mr. Damon Rowden, Mr. Kagiso Molefe, Mr. Chester McGensy III, Mr. Lee Hightower, Mr. Maurice Lewis, Ms. Adrienne Lalanne, Mr. Edward Sheppard, Mr. Pete Peterson, Mr. Irby Gaines, Mr. Johnny Sellers, Mr. Calvin Thomas, Mr. Kenneth Ramirez, Ms. Christina M. Brogden, and Mr. and Mrs. Bob and Mary Gavin. I thank all of you for your guidance. To my research participants, thank you for your commitment to tutoring. Finally, for all those whom I have forgotten to mention, thank you for your support.

CHAPTER I

THE RESEARCH PROBLEM

The objective of this research was to study in-home, one-on-one tutoring as a possible remedy for the inadequate education of African American males. In particular, I investigated African American males' perceptions of the relationship between a tutor and tutee within in-home, one-on-one tutoring. Several studies have been conducted on out-of-home, one-on-one tutoring (Bondy & Davis, 2000; Caserta-Henry, 1996; Hock et al., 2001). However, no research exists on the effects of the tutor-tutee caring relationship with African American males in in-home, one-on-one tutoring. To fill this gap in the research literature, my study explores seven African American males' perceptions of the tutor-tutee caring relationship within in-home, one-on-one tutoring.

Throughout this study, I have provided multiple examples from my past and current experience with in-home, one-on-one tutoring, my personal life experiences, and the perspectives of educational researchers in order to validate the need for my research. My research participants used their home language of Ebonics from their Delores Heights neighborhood of Jackson, California, to help express some of their thoughts (See Appendix F for sample Ebonics phrases). To protect the identity of my research participants, their parents, and the community in which they live (including teachers, community members, and schools), I use pseudonyms throughout this research.

Finally, I explain how some African American males have experienced inadequate education within the United States public school system, particularly the African American males whom I tutor from the Jackson Unified School District (JUSD), in order to set the stage for my research. Therefore, I am presenting my study of in-home, one-on-one tutoring as a potential remedy for the inadequate education of African American males. This book intends to provide insight into how some African American males may benefit from the relationship that is central to in-home, one-on-one tutoring.

Background and Need for the Study

For several years, I have worked as a tutor for one hundred African American males in the JUSD. Whenever I attend a class to observe my students, I take extensive notes regarding my students' behavior and their teachers' pedagogical styles. I often discuss with teachers the importance of using culturally related materials and pedagogical styles that reflect the culture of most African American males within their classrooms, including understanding the importance of teacher-student caring relationships. After observing and talking with teachers in general, I have found that most lack a general understanding of caring relationships within the context of the African American community, thus exacerbating the continuing problem of inadequate education for African American males. This experience prompted me to further investigate the history of inadequate education of African American males, with in-home, one-on-one tutoring as one possible solution.

The need for studying caring relationships between a tutor and tutee in in-home, one-on-one tutoring emerged from my review of recent research on inadequate education of African American males, including tracking, disproportional placement in special education, excessive suspensions, and high drop-out rates (California Department of Education, 2005; Kunjufu, 2005; Smiley, 2006). Kunjufu (2005) states that tracking is a way in which schools divide students into ability groups. Kunjufu argues that tracking can be destructive for low-achieving students, particularly African American males. He states, "...The rationale has been...students benefit from associating with their 'own kind'... it's frustrating for low-achieving students to be with high achievers" (p. 9). He further implies that tracking is a reflection of society, because those students who are divided into groups within the school system inevitably become an alienated population. He asserts that just as with class in U.S. society, students are eventually tracked into upper, middle, and lower ability groups.

Kunjufu (2005) propounds that many African American males are disproportionately placed into special education because of the contradictions among their teachers.

> Many students who are placed in special education are labeled ADD or ADHD. By stating that ADD is a medical disorder, experts place the burden and source of the problem on the child. Yet unlike other medical diseases such as diabetes or pneumonia, this is a disorder that pops up in one setting, only to disappear in another. Isn't it ironic that a Black boy may do just fine with one teacher, but in the next grade another teacher labels him hyperactive or with ADD? Is the problem with the boy or with an inconsistency between his teachers? (p. xi)

Kunjufu's (2005) statement reflects the reality of the African American males whom I tutor. Most of my students are labeled with Attention Deficit Disorder (ADD) or Attention Deficit Hyperactive Disorder (ADHD), and many of their teachers and parents disagree in how they view my students.

Smiley (2006) reports "One out of three African American students in seventh through twelfth grades has been suspended or expelled at some point, as opposed to 15 percent of white children" (p. 33). This fact is similar to the situations many of my tutees encounter in JUSD. Research on high drop-out rates among African American males in California reveals more incidents of inadequate education. The California Department of Education (CDOE) 2005-2006 drop-out rate statistics for Grades 9-12 show that African Americans have a higher four-year drop-out rate at 24.3% compared to white students at 8.2%. These statistics paint a daunting and dismal picture of the current educational state of African American males in California, and represent some of the African American males I tutor in the JUSD. Therefore, it is imperative that alternative solutions to inadequate education, such as in-home, one-on-one tutoring, be investigated to help decrease excessive suspensions, tracking, disproportionate placement in special education, and high drop-out rates.

Statement of the Problem

Effective teachers and tutors who demonstrate caring relationships can have a positive impact on African American males. These relationships founded on mutual trust can yield increased effort and performance from all participants (such as teacher-student or tutor-tutee). These relationships are demonstrated by coaches, teachers, tutors, and after-school staff (Dance, 2002; Katz, 1999; Ladson-Billings, 1994; Valenzuela, 1999). In her research with Latino immigrants, Katz (1999) proposes that caring is essential to student achievement, especially when teachers and students are from different neighborhoods and cultural backgrounds. Although her research does not address African American males, it further validates the need to investigate the effects of a tutor-tutee caring relationship on African American males' student achievement within in-home, one-on-one tutoring.

Similarly, Ladson-Billings (1994) discusses how the care of coaches helps motivate students to learn. She declares, "...coaches also believe their students are capable of excellence, but they are comfortable sharing the responsibility to help them achieve it with parents, community members, and the students themselves..." (p. 24). Her depiction of coaches helps highlight the power of caring.

In the same manner, Ladson-Billings (1994) discusses the importance of teacher care by describing the relationships teachers establish with students.

> ...teachers can also be identified by the ways in which they structure their social interactions. Their relationships with students are fluid and equitable and extend beyond the classroom. They demonstrate a connectedness with all of their students and encourage that same connectedness between the students. They encourage a community of learners; they encourage their students to learn collaboratively. (p. 25)

The author's point clarifies the importance of teacher-student care by further illuminating some ways to help African American males succeed in education.

In *Subtractive Schooling*, Valenzuela (1999) describes the characteristics of an effective teacher named Mr. Lundgren:

He gives every student a chance to rewrite the assignment if they want to try for a higher grade...In some cases, Mr. Lundgren gives his Spanish-dominant students the opportunity to do the assignment in Spanish. He mentioned a female student whose poor English-language skills would have made the paper assignment overwhelming...Mr. Lundgren regularly counsels students, advising all-and convincing a few-that to be good mechanics, they need math and that to be able to run their own shops, they need to be able to read and write well. (p. 103)

Valenzuela's account provides a clear representation of a caring teacher.

Dance's (2002) research on teacher-student relationships helps validate claims for the effectiveness of caring. Dance shows that teachers who exhibited a high level of care had an encouraging effect on the African American males whom she tutored and mentored. She reports "students with actual...ties to street culture tended to gravitate toward...teachers who...established a reputation for being caring" (p. 45). Dance further describes this caring relationship as teachers having a good sense of humor, making learning fun and enjoyable for the students, and believing in the students.

Dance (2002) describes how students respect what she refers to as "down" teachers:

"Down" teachers are not just teachers, they are also mentors and friends. Most important, "down" teachers take the time to get to know and understand their students. When I asked students if there was anything they would change about school, implicit in many of their responses was a call for more teachers who are "down". (p. 47)

In this way, caring can be further operationalized from the perspective of young African American males, such as my tutees.

Conversely, the lack of teacher care can have a negative impact on African American males' education (Kunjufu, 2002; Ladson-Billings, 1994). Ladson-Billings asserts that some teachers in her study demonstrated a lack of care for Black students through their racist attitudes. The author retells a conversation between a master teacher, supposedly one of the district's finest, and a student teacher in the cafeteria.

The cooperating teacher...tells the student teacher that she will have to be especially careful to recognize that there are two types of black students in the school. She observes that there are "white-blacks" and "black-blacks." The white-blacks are easy to deal with because they come from "good' homes and have "white" values. But the black-blacks are less capable academically and have behavior problems. As the student teacher listens she is shocked by what her cooperating teacher is saying but she is even more shocked that none of the other teachers in the lounge appears to find what's being said unusual. (p. 20)

Ladson-Billings' (1994) research is crucial to understanding how lack of care, in this case demonstrated by a racist teacher, can construe the perception of Black students. Her research on public school teachers relates to my research with African American males and in-home, one-on-one tutoring because this racist practice is often played out in the urban schools the students attend.

In his work on teacher training, Kunjufu (2002) details the difficulty in encouraging uncaring white teachers to increase their effort with Black children in public schools. He reports one training in which he was asked by a principal to help educate his staff on racial transition,

The principal invited me to speak to the teachers to give them strategies on how to maximize the achievement of African American students. The problem was that the teachers viewed the students as 'these children' and felt that I needed to fix the children and their parents. They felt nothing needed modification on their part... (p. 20)

Kunjufu's research illuminates how some uncaring teachers believe the problem lies solely within the home of the African American males, absolving themselves from any responsibility.

Several research studies have shown the overall academic value of a tutoring relationship (Beyth-Marom et al., 2001; Bondy & Davis, 2000; Caserta-Henry, 1996; Hock et al., 2001). Bondy and Davis (2000) found that tutors were able to overcome certain relationship difficulties with their students after they exhibited a level of care toward their students. The authors affirm that students become more interested in the subject being taught to them when tutors demonstrate a level of care.

Caserta-Henry (1996) states that first graders improved their spelling tests as well as written and observation skills when paired with high school reading buddies. These first graders also developed a more positive attitude towards reading and writing. Hock et al. (2001) pointed out that junior high school students can increase their quiz and test scores through one-on-one tutoring. Moreover, Beyth-Marom et al. (2001) assert that home tutoring is more preferable than being tutored in the community because students are able to comprehend the subject more effortlessly. They enjoy the home environment more and find it also increases their level of concentration.

Purpose of the Study

As shown above, several studies have been conducted on out-of-home, one-on-one tutoring (Bondy & Davis, 2000; Caserta-Henry, 1996; Hock et al., 2001). However, there is no research on the effects of the tutor-tutee caring relationship with African American males with the context of in-home, one-on-one tutoring. To fill this gap in the research literature, my study explored African American males' perceptions of the tutor-tutee caring relationship within in home, one-on-one tutoring. My participants were seven African American males who are currently being tutored within their home and at an individual level. I used a qualitative approach to engage my participants in a dialogue regarding their experiences with this type of tutoring. This involved one individual face-to-face conversation between the researcher and the participants.

Research Questions

1. What are the teacher-student relationships and academic experiences of African American males in a public school setting?

2. What are the tutor-tutee relationships and academic experiences of African American males in an in-home, one-on-one tutorial situation?

3. How do students compare their relationships and academic experiences in public school with in-home, one-on-one tutoring?

4. What recommendations would students make for improving in-home tutoring?

Theoretical Rationale

In this section, I elaborate the several theoretical frameworks that guide my research study. I describe how Ladson-Billings and Tate's (1995) discussion of critical race theory gives insight to understanding the inadequate education experiences of African American males in public schools. I also explain how Coleman's (1990) concept of social capital and Stanton-Salazar's (1997) use of this concept frame my study of African American males. Finally, I use Vygotsky's (1978) Zone of Proximal Development (ZPD) theory to understand how a tutor-tutee caring relationship may increase the academic performance among African American males.

Critical Race Theory

Ladson-Billings and Tate (1995) suggest social inequity in general and school inequity in particular are based on three essential concepts:

1. Race continues to be a significant factor in determining inequity in the United States.

2. U.S. society is based on property rights.

3. The intersection of race and property creates an analytic tool through which we can understand social (and, consequently, school) inequity. (p. 48)

The heart of their analysis of racism in education lies in their statement, "we argue that the cause of their poverty in conjunction with the condition of their schools and schooling is institutional and structural racism" (p. 55). This points to the fact that African American males' inadequate education is rooted in the structure of U.S. society.

Coleman's Concept of Social Capital

Coleman (1990) delineates social capital as resources obtained by actors of any given group within a society who exhibit a level of trust among each other that helps keep the group intact. This trust must be mutually beneficial to all members of that group. Coleman further clarifies:

Social capital is defined by its function. It is not a single entity, but a variety of different entities having two characteristics in common: They all consist of some aspect of a social structure, and they facilitate certain actions of individuals who are within the structure. Like other forms of capital, social capital is productive, making possible the achievement of certain ends that would not be attainable in its absence. (p. 302)

Coleman's description of social capital is pertinent to my work with in-home, one-on-one tutoring because it provides a lens through which to explore the importance of a caring relationship between tutor-tutee.

Stanton-Salazar's Application of Social Capital

In discussing institutional support, Stanton-Salazar (1997) argues that these support systems established within mainstream institutions are needed for social growth, school success, and status achievement:

> ...key forms of social support that function to help children and adolescents become effective participants within mainstream institutional spheres, particularly the school system. Such support enables young people to become successful consumers and entrepreneurs within mainstream marketplace, to manage effectively the stresses of participating in mainstream settings, and, in general, to exercise greater control over their lives and their futures. (p. 10)

Stanton-Salazar highlights the importance of relationships established between teachers and students in educational institutions. These relationships often help the students navigate the tumultuous politics within mainstream education institutions.

Vygotsky's Zone of Proximal Development Theory

Vygotsky's (1978) Zone of Proximal Development affords a lens to guide my research into the educational processes of African American males within in-home, one-on-one tutoring and provide possible tools to develop other similar tutorial programs. Most significantly, Vygotsky posits that learning is more than the acquisition of the ability to think and acquire skills. He believes knowledge comes from the ability to learn many concepts through a variety of educational techniques and social interaction.

The essence of Vygotsky's (1978) Zone of Proximal Development lies in the learning process developed in a relationship between a child and a more advanced peer or adult. It is within this interaction that a child attains understanding. He describes, "...learning awakens a variety of internal developmental processes that are able to operate only when the child is interacting with people in his environment and in cooperation with his peers" (p. 90). For this reason, a caring relationship is one key factor in the academic development of a child. Thus, one can argue that tutor-tutee caring relationships established within in-home, one-on-one tutoring can increase the academic development of African American males.

In closing, Critical Race Theory, Social Capital Theory, and Zone of Proximal Development Theory all set the theoretical foundation for my research on in-home, one-on-one tutoring. Critical Race Theory has revealed that African American children's poor living and school conditions result from structural and institutional racism. Social Capital Theory gives insight into how students are able to obtain social capital from establishing caring relationships with their teachers or agents from educational institutions. Finally, Zone of Proximal Development Theory clarifies how a caring relationship may potentially increase the academic achievement among African American males within in-home, one-on-one tutoring.

Limitations of the Study

Because I am the tutor of the participants in this study, this research may reflect my subjectivity. Additionally, due to the small sample size of seven African American males and the non-random nature of sampling, the findings from the study are not generalizable. The stories that were told by the student participants and parents were just that - their stories, their experiences, and ultimately their voices. Their stories did not necessarily express the voices and experiences of all African American males.

Significance of the Study

No research exists in the area of African American males' perceptions of the importance of the tutor-tutee relationship within in-home, one-on-one tutoring. This study contributed not only to this knowledge base and to basic research on educating African American males, but also brought forth new knowledge concerning tutor-tutee caring relationships within in-home, one-on-one tutoring. This original qualitative study provides a model to help researchers, parents, and administrators who might be interested in developing future in-home, one-on-one tutoring programs. Furthermore, this research gives insights to educators and parents who are looking for creative ways to remedy the inadequate education of African American males, specifically those in urban schools.

Organization of the Book

I have organized this book into six chapters. The reason for this structure is to present the findings in two chapters: profiles of the participants in Chapter IV and the findings from the research questions in Chapter V. I did this because I did not want my participants to get lost amidst the data. In addition, I wanted to give enough space to their backgrounds so that the reader can fully understand their lives.

CHAPTER II

REVIEW OF THE LITERATURE

In this literature review, I present research on: (a) inadequate education of African American males, (b) caring relationships, and (c) tutoring. The intent of this literature review is to frame this particular study within educational research and to expose the existing gaps in that research.

Inadequate Education of African American Males

Research on the inadequate education of African American males reveals their lack of progress in the United States. From a historical context, African Americans tried to attain education after slavery, but faced many roadblocks that prevented them from receiving an adequate education. Court cases reveal attempts to remedy the inadequate education of African Americans, but most have failed to sustain progress. Research on African American males in schools today exposes some hope, but also shows how they continue to battle disparaging circumstances.

The following statistics paint a very dismal picture of the aforementioned:

1. Fifty-five percent of African American males graduate from high school compared to seventy-five of White males.

2. Ten percent of the nation's African American students are enrolled in two of the largest urban districts, New York and Chicago, the same school districts that fail to graduate seventy percent of these students (Schott Foundation for Public Education, 2006).

These statistics shed light on the lack of parity in educational achievement between Blacks and their white counterparts that ultimately translates into disparities in employment, wages, and health. Low educational attainment dramatically undermines the successful transition of young African American males into adulthood and their potential to contribute to the society. They continue to be disproportionately represented in the juvenile justice system and experience high rates of unemployment (Schott Foundation for Public Education, 2006).

Before discussing inadequate education of African American males in the United States, we must begin with a synopsis of when African Americans were first notified of their freedom. After slavery, many African Americans were still denied their inalienable rights of freedom, including the right to be educated. Their obstruction from education was due for the most part to racial hierarchy and White American domination (Anderson, 1988; Bennett, 2003). In the early 1860's, President Abraham Lincoln issued his renowned Emancipation Proclamation. Initially, this document was weak and vague because it allowed Blacks freedom in the southern states, where Lincoln had no power, and lacked specifics on the implementation process involving Blacks' freedom.

This unclear document set the tone for the enactment of the Black Codes which represented a formidable way to discourage free Black citizens from participating in voting, employment, and education. Bennett (2003) defines the codes as illegal rules that southern Whites used to restrict Blacks to farming and other menial employment opportunities. For instance, one code involved armed White men patrolling the South harassing free Backs and killing them. Hundreds of freed Blacks were murdered in riots by policemen and other government officials. In describing Whites' cruelty and racial categorization of Blacks during this time, Bennett recounts, "You kill a Negro, they do not deem murder; to debauch a Negro woman, they do not think fornication; to take property away from a Negro, they do not consider robbery..." (p. 207).

Whites' insistence on a segregated school system can be understood through Anderson's (1998) comment that in the early 1800's, the South made it illegal to teach enslaved children how to read and write. Even though laws were passed to emancipate slaves, the existing public school system continued to exclude freed slaves and their children. Due to the hostility towards free education for ex-slaves, White planters resisted the movement for education among Blacks by establishing Black codes and Jim Crow laws which made it difficult to enter the public school system. For instance, some southern states enacted vagrancy laws, which Anderson states "gave local authorities a virtual mandate to arrest any poor man who did not have a labor contract" (p. 25). These laws forced Blacks to go back to work for their White masters, thus eliminating any future plans to become educated.

Anderson's (1988) examination of Black southern education provides an exceptional analysis and validation of how the categorization of race was a significant factor in the segregation of newly freed African Americans. He details the struggles of African Americans who try to obtain education during and after slavery, while sustaining their survival in a racist white supremacist society. The author reveals that racial categorization continues to be a mechanism used by whites to keep African Americans segregated and conquered.

As Anderson (1988) explains, the continuous plan by the racist South was to hinder the achievement of education for most African Americans during slavery. He explains "Between 1800 and 1835, most southern states enacted legislation making it a crime to teach enslaved children to read" (p. 2). This example of education obstruction speaks to the initial organization of how most whites used the legal system to enact racist laws that validated discrimination against Blacks. In response, the education of some African Americans during and after slavery was taught, provided, and established by African Americans. The author discusses "...ex-slaves initiated and sustained schools...Sabbath schools...operated mainly in the evenings and on weekends, provided basic literacy instruction" (p. 12). Black education is a testimony to Black self-empowerment and autonomy.

U.S. Supreme Court and other key court cases give a broader picture of how African Americans were continually segregated in education and yet attempted to decrease this segregation (*Plessy v. Ferguson, 1896*; *Brown v. Board of Education, 1954).* Prior to the well-known *Brown v. Board of Education (1954)* case was the *Plessy v. Ferguson* case *(1896).*

In 1892 Homer Plessy, a citizen of Louisiana who was one-eighth black and seven-eighths white, was placed under arrest for riding in a white-only car during an intrastate trip. The event had been planned by a group of renowned African Americans from New Orleans – mainly Creoles, or French-speaking people of mixed ethnicity. Their ride was a direct confrontation to the Louisiana statute requiring railway companies to provide separate and equivalent lodging for whites and blacks. The constitutional issue in discussion was the right of a state to make and implement this kind of racial discrimination. Prior to this case, Louisiana, along with other southern states, passed white supremacy laws, which extended from the private to public realm under state mandate and enforcement (Martin, 1998).

In 1892, the Supreme Court defended these laws, including the Louisiana Jim Crow railway statute. This decision declared that separate and equal provisions for Blacks and whites were consistent with the equal protection clause of the Fourteenth Amendment. The decision also represented race as a normal, not random, classification for the description of state-defined rights (Martin, 1998). Subsequently, *Brown v. Board of Education (1954)* overturned this racist law.

On May 17, 1954, *Brown v. Board of Education* overturned *Plessy v. Ferguson (1896)* in the United States Supreme Court. The courts ruled that segregating children by race violated the Equal Protection Clause of the Fourteenth Amendment, regardless of the physical facilities and other elements of the schools. The case overturned the doctrine of separate but equal schools on the grounds of being unconstitutional. The decision reversed the Court's 1896 decision in *Plessy v. Ferguson,* which had sustained the concept and practice of state-endorsed racial discrimination, otherwise known as Jim Crow – the illusion of separate but equal public accommodations and organizations for blacks and whites.

Fifty years after *Brown* when the United States Supreme Court ruled segregation as illegal, most Black children still attend public schools where they represent the majority of the student body; thus segregation prevails today (Gordon, 2006). Several factors have led to the disparity in the academic achievement of African American males, including high drop-out rates, special education enrollments, racism, and negative perceptions (Cooper & Jordan, 2002; Kunjufu, 2005; Ladson-Billings, 1994; Noguera, 2005; Schott Foundation for Public Education, 2006). Ladson-Billings (1994) depicts the high drop-out and suspension rates among African American children.

> African American children are three times as likely to drop out of school as white children are and twice as likely to be suspended from school. The high school drop out rate in New York and California is about 35 percent; in inner cities, where large numbers of African American students live, the rate nears 50 percent. African American students make up only about 17 percent of the public school population but 41 percent of the special-education population. These dismal statistics hold despite the two waves of educational reform initiated in the 1980s. (p. 2)

Kunjufu (2005) reports Black males are disproportionately placed in special education, clarifying the continuing problem of inadequate education. He claims, "Only 27 percent of African American male special education students graduate from high school. Only 41 percent of African American male regular students graduate from high school" (p. 14). Kunjufu suggests that many African American boys are more often placed in special education because they are misdiagnosed. Many teachers view them as uncontrollable. For this reason, many teachers, principals, and counselors perceive African American males as candidates for special education.

Kunjufu (2005) also declares "African American students comprise 17 percent of public school students but constitute only 3 percent of gifted and talented students, African American males, less than 1 percent" (p. 18). Kunjufu states that racial discrimination is a primary cause of Black males being placed in special education. He writes, "What is the reason why African American males have a 3.26 greater chance of being labeled mentally retarded than White females, a 2.34 greater chance being placed in an LD classroom, and an astronomical 5.52 greater chance of being placed in an emotionally disturbed classroom" (p. 21). These statistics further illustrate the current reality of African American males in schools today.

The Schott Foundation for Public Education (2006) reports that Oakland Unified School district (OUSD) in 2002 had 36.56 percent of their African American males labeled as mentally retarded compared to 3.23 percent of white males. OUSD also had a 44.87 percentage of suspensions among African American males compared to 1.57 among white males. In addition, the Schott Foundation for Public Education discusses the varying degree of inadequate education within the school district. The organization reports, "Black male students are significantly under-represented in Gifted/Talented programs and over-represented in Mental Retardation classifications, as well as out-of-school suspensions" (p. 21).

Kunjufu (2005) claims that most teachers ignore, misunderstand, and are unaware of the power of race in educating African American males. In describing a teacher in Seattle, Washington, where he was assigned to train a group of teachers, Kunjufu explains how this teacher was completely unaware.

> ...she did not see color. She saw children as children...So I asked if I could visit her classroom...Her students were a mosaic of the country: 60 percent African American, 20 percent Asian and Hispanic, and 20 percent White. Yet she had an all-White Dick and Jane bulletin board, library collection, and lesson plans. The only color she saw was white. (p. 19)

Similarly, Noguera (2005) describes an experience with a high school student in the Bay Area. An African American male student had approached him with concerns about a paper he was writing for another professor on the novel *Huckleberry Finn*. The student was upset because despite the frequent use of the word "nigger" throughout the text, students in this particular class were asked to leave out race because it was not an important point of the story. The student was angry because he felt he had no alternatives except to turn in what the teacher expected. Both incidents by Kunjufu (2005) and Noguera (2005) make clear the issue of racism to which most African American males must succumb in mainstream education.

Noguera (2005) declares that African American male athletes are likely to be perceived as nonacademic by their teachers. He claims,

> For African American males, who are more likely than any other group to be subjected to negative forms of treatment in school, the message is clear: Individuals of their race and gender may excel in sports, but not in math or history. (p. 63)

Noguera further explains that Black males are most often located in school, in detention, special education, or in sports. This compartmentalization leads to the negative perception that Blacks are unable to compete in the science club or write for the school newspaper.

These current statistics on African American males concerning high drop-out rates, special education enrollments, racism, and negative perceptions give just a small portrait of inadequate education. Statistics show the urgent need for ongoing research into solutions for the inadequate education of African American males. Despite these incidences of inadequate education, serious efforts to educate African American males have been made, including school- and community-based programs (Dance, 2002; Fashola, 2005; Kunjufu, 2005; Smiley, 2006).

Fashola (2005) provides examples of after-school programs that have adequately educated African American males. Howard Street Tutoring program focuses on improving the academic outcomes of low-performing students. The program recruits volunteers from college campuses who tutor second and third grade students in reading. Once a day, students engage in one hour daily reading sessions with a volunteer. Results show that reading scores have increased among African American males who attend.

In her study of African American males, Dance (2002) documents the success of the Paul Robeson Institute for Positive Self-Development. This organization is a supplemental school program created in Boston by African American men. The organization's primary goal is to provide African American teachers and mentors for young Black boys. The success of the institute, from the perspective of the youth, is based upon the way the teachers interact with the youth.

Fine (2002) discusses a program started by the 100 Black Men of America organization called the Wimberly Initiative. Fine describes one of the programs involving African American male professionals and retirees in Charlotte, North Carolina. She writes that these African American males visit elementary schools to mentor and tutor young African American males afterschool. Sometimes these African American male professionals and retirees supervise children on field trips and support principals with disciplinary procedures. In his research on the Wimberly Initiative, Kunjufu (2005) reports that this program was founded to decrease the amount of African American males being placed in special education. The overall goal of the organization is to provide role models and support for African American males in the public school system. The approach includes:

1. Professional development for staff, including diversity training.
2. A parent-directed program to assist families to better represent their sons in IEP meetings.
3. A twice-weekly after-school program to improve academic, behavioral, and social skills of students.
4. Individual mentoring of Black boys. (p. 183)

Smiley (2006) presents several programs for improving the education of African Americans. One program was started by an elderly woman named Ms. Thelma Harrison, a leader of the Civil Rights Movement, who reads to pre-school children. He accounts, "With the skills these young children acquire under Harrison's tutelage, they are prepared to succeed in their early years of elementary school...She has developed relationships with parents, grandparents, teachers, and administrators..." (p. 35).

Another project, the Children's Defense Fund Freedom Schools, helps establish after-school programs in churches, schools, and community organizations across the United States in different communities. Smiley (2006) notes, "The program's key elements are educational achievement and cultural awareness, parental involvement, intergenerational leadership, community involvement, and social action" (p. 37).

Big Brothers/Big Sisters is another program that has attempted to educate African American males (Fashola, 2005). The goal of the program, originally founded by the United States Department of Justice, is to screen potential volunteers who are then placed with children from single-parent homes. These volunteers are responsible for teaching children how to make healthy lifestyle decisions and to provide them with positive experiences that will help them navigate through later life challenges.

On average, the volunteers spend at least four to six hours a month with their little brothers and sisters. Fashola (2005) quotes, "Although this program was not specifically designed to serve African American males exclusively...the goals and outcomes of this program should be emulated by other organizations intending to improve social and behavioral skills of African American males" (p. 33). A study of the program revealed that students were less likely to use drugs or participate in gangs and more likely to improve their peer relationships after being involved with the program.

Caring Relationships

Noddings (1992) depicts the process of caring in the following way:

> Caring, in both its natural and ethical senses, describes a certain kind of relation. It is one in which one person, A, the carer, cares for another, B, and B recognizes that A cares for B. As described earlier, A's consciousness during the interval of caring is marked by (1) engrossment or nonselective attention, and (2) motivational displacement or the desire to help. A genuinely listens, feels, and responds with honest concern for B's expressed interests or needs. When we say, 'B recognizes,' we mean that B receives A's caring and reacts in a way that shows it. A relation of caring is complete when B's recognition becomes part of what A receives in his or her attentiveness. (p. 91)

Noddings' contextualization of a caring relationship provides comprehensive meaning and lays the foundation for other types of care to be generated by researchers.

Furthermore, Noddings (1992) defines a caring relation as:

> a connection or encounter between two human beings – a carer and a recipient of care, or cared-for...A failure on the part of either carer or cared-for blocks completion of caring... No matter how hard teachers try to care, if the caring is not received by students, the claim 'they don't care' has some validity. It suggest that something is very wrong. (p. 15)

Noddings' description gives emphasis to the symbiotic relationship that is inherent in a caring relation. Thereby, two people are responsible for the implementation of care (e.g., teacher-student/ tutor-tutee).

Focusing on African American males, Fashola (2005) asserts that they can benefit from being exposed to good teachers, especially African American male teachers. She writes that schools must critically reflect on the educator responsible for teaching African American males:

> Many of the students who are training to be educators have little, if any, experience interacting with racially and culturally different students. Although there is no substitute for effective school organization, curriculum, and programs of professional development, the question of who teaches African American boys is as critical to the academic success of these students as what is taught and how it is presented. (p. 10)

Fashola highlights the importance of teacher-student caring with African American males in mainstream classrooms. This section on caring relationships attempts to clarify how the notion of caring may positively affect the academic performance of African American males within in-home, one-on-one tutoring.

Ladson-Billings (1994), Dance (2002), and Gay (2005) all define the essentials and the effects of a caring relationship between teachers and students with examples of caring teachers. Dance (2002) reveals that African American males show more interest in school once they have a teacher who cares. When African American males trust that their teachers are caring, they will reciprocate with an effort of commitment to school. Dance gives a detailed definition of caring:

From student interviews and field observations, I developed a typology of three types of teachers encountered by students in my study: (1) uncaring/unempathetic teachers, the teachers who seem not to care about students in general and who do not understand the streets in particular; (2) caring/unempathetic teachers, who care about students in general, but do not understand the streets in particular; (3) caring/empathetic teachers, who care about students in general and understand-or care enough to learn about-the streets in particular, that is, teachers who are considered "down" by street-savvy youth. (p. 46)

Similarly, Ladson-Billings (1994) asserts that a caring relationship is embodied in teachers who practice culturally relevant pedagogy. This enables students to see their reality represented within the curriculum. Teachers who want to increase the academic achievement of children must extend their work beyond the classroom, as she describes:

They demonstrate a connectedness with all of their students and encourage a community of learners; they encourage their students to learn collaboratively. Finally, such teachers are identified by their notions of knowledge. They believe that knowledge is continuously re-created, recycled, and shared by teachers and students alike. (p. 25)

Ladson-Billings' description helps clarify the commitment needed to cultivate and maintain a caring relationship with students.

Caring relationships also can have a positive effect on pedagogy. Gay (2005) argues that teachers should develop a social and interpersonal relationship with their students to convey a sense of personal kinship. In addition, she contends that a "culturally responsive pedagogy should integrate a sense of connectedness, care, and cultural support for students of color, specifically Blacks, Native Americans, Latino, and Asian students" (p. 234). The content of teaching should be personally meaningful to the student, allowing for a cultivation of social and cultural consciousness to occur. Gay illustrates how improved pedagogy should be one of America's urgent priorities. A socially responsive pedagogy gives action to both a social and politically arena that has downplayed Blacks throughout the history of their education. Gay's work can be used by educators to create a culturally relevant pedagogy that is receptive to the specific needs of African American males.

Tutoring

In order to comprehend the field of tutoring, several studies expose a broad range of tutoring methods which include in-school, after-school, and in-home. Some studies describe the process of in-school tutoring (Madden & Slavin, 2001; Yogev & Ronen, 1982). Yogev and Ronen (1982) conducted a year-long study on the effects of a tutor training program on high school freshmen. The sample consisted of 73 freshmen who participated in the tutor training program compared to 98 other freshmen. The results showed that the training program increased the students' empathy, altruism, and self-esteem. Madden and Slavin (2001) studied the effects of their program, Success for All (SFA), which involves one-on-one peer-assisted reading and teacher-assisted reading. The results show that students are able to gain the necessary attention needed to build on their particular reading limitations because of the one-on-one component.

Few studies document the process of after-school tutoring (Bondy & Davis; 2000, Hock et al., 2001). Bondy and Davis (2000) studied white middle-class pre-service teachers and their relationships with African American students in Florida Housing Projects. The authors found that when a tutor exhibits a certain level of care for the students, students become more interested in the subject being taught.

Hock et al. (2001) investigated the effects of an after-school tutorial program on three junior high school students labeled "at-risk" and "learning disabled." They were tutored by University students for two to three hours a week for approximately 45 minutes of instruction. The results revealed that students could earn a score of average or better on quizzes and tests with the support of qualified adult tutors. The authors also found that tutors could teach students learning techniques when practicing homework assignments. In addition, the researchers found that students continued to use these learning techniques after tutoring. This study used Vygotsky's (1978) theory of ZPD in that the core of the students' success was the interaction between a student and a more advanced peer or adult (e.g., the students from the University).

Two studies compared in-home tutoring with in-school and community-based tutoring (Beyth-Marom et al., 2001; Hook & DuPaul, 1999). Hook and DuPaul (1999) studied four elementary public school students with Attention Deficit Hyperactivity Disorder (ADHD) who were tutored by their parents at home and tutored by their teachers at school. The study compared reading skill improvements in school and at home. The results showed that most students' reading scores improved within a home setting as well as a school environment. Thereby, students benefit by learning in the environment of the home as well at school.

Beyth-Marom et al.'s (2001) study involved 600 college students who registered for a tutorial class at the Open University of Israel. The students were offered group, face-to-face tutoring in their local neighborhoods, tutoring via satellite broadcasting to students around the country, and tutoring at home using the same satellite program on the television or computer screen. This study examined the differences among students tutored in these different environments. The results revealed that the students preferred the neighborhood tutoring the least and satellite home tutorials the most. Data showed that the satellite home tutoring was the most acceptable because students were able to comprehend the subject more effortlessly; students enjoyed the home environment more since it increased their level of concentration.

Summary

Research on the history of inadequate education of African American males reveals a discouraging picture. Even after the end of slavery in the 1860s, Blacks were excluded from quality integrated schools until *Brown v. Board of Education* overturned *Plessy* in 1954. However, although court cases like *Brown* legally promoted desegregation, segregation and inadequate education still prevail today. As explained earlier, this situation can be analyzed through Critical Race Theory as due to structural and institutional racism (Ladson-Billings & Tate, 1995).

Particularly with students who are marginalized in school, like African American males, literature (Dance, 2002; Fashola, 2005) shows that caring relationships with teachers are essential to their academic success. Ladson-Billings (1994), Dance (2002), and Gay (2005) all state that to demonstrate caring, teachers must make effort to go beyond the classroom or do whatever it takes to build empathy with and interest in the students' culture.

Literature on tutoring has revealed the positive effects of out-of-home tutoring programs for all students, particularly in increasing academic skills. Although one study (Bondy & Davis, 2000) examined the role of caring in an after-school tutoring relationship between teachers and African American students, not one single study has focused on the impact of tutor-tutee caring relationships within in-home tutoring.

Therefore, my study addresses this gap in the research literature. The objective was to explore the tutor-tutee relationship within in-home, one-on-one tutoring through the perceptions of African American males. This study is unique in two important ways: the context is one-on-one, in-home tutoring, and it embraces the students' perspectives of their own learning. Furthermore, this study embodies the Vygotskyan (1978) principle of Zone of Proximal Development: a student learns best in social interaction with an adult or a more capable peer.

CHAPTER III

METHODOLOGY

The purpose of this study was to explore African American males' perceptions of the tutor-tutee caring relationship within in-home, one-on-one tutoring. My participants were seven African American males who currently attend in-home, one-on-one tutoring and urban public schools. The objective was to inquire into participants' perceptions through one face-to-face interview using open-ended questions.

Qualitative Research Design

Within a qualitative research paradigm, I used a phenomenological research approach in my study because I analyzed the perceptions of the participants. Creswell (2003) outlines certain criteria for phenomenological research. He suggests, "the researcher identifies the 'essence' of human experiences concerning a phenomenon, as described by participants in a study. Understanding the 'lived experiences' marks phenomenology as a philosophy as well as a method..." (p. 15). Because of my relationship with the participants as their tutor, I was able to observe them in public school and during tutoring. During these observations, I was able to note shared experiences of inadequate education in which I identified lack of care as the core of these incidents. In this chapter, I discuss the general process of qualitative research, including my research setting, questions, data analysis, ethical considerations of my study, and methodological reflections.

Research Setting

The research was conducted in the homes of my participants. Because I have a reputation as an effective tutor, my students' parents allowed me to conduct research with their children. The families see me as a trusted member of the community and their particular neighborhoods. I have a personal connection to the students' communities because we share similar values, belief systems, and the language of Ebonics.

All of my students live in Delores Heights, a community downtrodden with poverty, drugs, and negative environmental impacts possibly caused by the United States Naval Shipyard and the Pacific, Gas, and Electric Company (PG&E) plant's history of alleged leakages. Ester and Harrison (2004) state that 48% of Delores Heights residents are African American. Since the appearance of the Naval Shipyard and the PG&E plant, the Delores Heights community has been severely damaged by their pollutants. Both companies have deposited dangerous contaminants around the community, such as leaking underground fuel tanks and hazardous waste. These pollutants have caused a variety of diseases, including asthma, breast cancer, and high rates of infant mortality. The authors also posit that Delores Heights is the fifth highest community for children with lead poisoning.

Nearly 40% of the Delores Heights residents have an annual income below $15,000 with a 13% percent unemployment rate, almost twice the unemployment rate for the entire city. In addition, Ester and Harrison (2004) claim "The health of the local residents has been heavily impacted by the ongoing environmental contamination of the community's soil and water with particles, pesticides, petrochemicals..." (p. 5). These current facts paint a daunting but realistic picture of the Delores Heights community, the home of my students.

Participants

I used a purposive sample for my research. The seven African American males in my study were chosen according to their interest and willingness to discuss openly their perceptions of tutor-tutee caring relationships (See Chapter IV for Participant Profiles).

Data Collection

I conducted a four-step data collection process which included: (a) conducting a one-hour face-to-face dialogue with my participants on their perceptions of tutor-tutee caring relationships using open-ended questions, (b) transcribing all the dialogues, (c) participants reviewing the transcripts for validity, and (d) revising the transcriptions according to their feedback. All the interviews took place in the homes of my participants during the month of June 2008.

I conducted and transcribed two interviews per week. The week following each interview, I verified the authenticity of my transcriptions with each participant. To triangulate, I utilized the field notes that I recorded immediately after each tutoring session in my researcher's journal. Embedded in these field notes were my reflections on the tutees. These field notes also included the parents' commentary on their children's education in public schools. I recorded their actual words as best as I could recount.

Interview Questions

The interview process was guided by four broad research questions. Following are the research questions and the probing questions under each.

Research Question #1: What are the teacher-student relationships and academic experiences of African American males in a public school setting?

Interview Questions

A. What do you think about all of your experiences in school?

(Ask the interviewee to specify previous and present years in school)

- Why do you think that?

B. What are the reasons you go to school in the first place?

C. How do you feel during class? Why do you feel that way?

D. How do you feel after school has ended everyday? Why do you feel that way?

E. How do you feel about your teachers?

(Then after answer: what makes you feel that way?)

F. How do you feel your teachers want you to do in school? How do you know that?

- In what ways does he/she demonstrate this?

Research Question #2: What are the tutor-tutee relationships and academic experiences of African American males in an in-home, one-on-one tutorial situation?

Interview Questions:

A. What do you think about all of your experiences in tutoring?

(Ask the interviewee to specify previous and present years in tutoring)

- Why do you think that?

B. What are the reasons you have a tutor in the first place?

C. How do you feel during tutoring session? Why do you feel that way?

D. How do you feel after tutoring has ended everyday? Why do you feel that way?

E. How do you feel about your tutor?

(Then after answer: what makes you feel that way?)

F. How do you feel your tutor wants you to do in school? How do you know that?

Research Question #3: How do students compare their relationships and academic experiences in public school with in-home, one-on-one tutoring?

Interview Questions:

A. How do you compare your relationships with your teacher to your relationships with your tutor?

- What makes you feel that way?

B. How do you compare your academic experiences in public school with your academic experiences in in-home, one-on-one tutoring?

- What makes you feel that way?

Research Question #4: What recommendations would students make for improving in-home tutoring?

Interview Questions

A. What things have been helpful for you in your tutoring?

B. What things would you change about tutoring to make it even better?

C. In what ways can your tutor improve his/her tutoring?

Data Analysis

After collecting data from the interviews, I analyzed the data by critically reflecting, note taking, and codifying what Creswell (2003) calls "chunks" of data. Data analysis was an ongoing process, including continual reflection, asking analytical questions, and writing notes throughout the study. It involved using open-ended data and asking general questions from the information provided by the participants.

More specifically, I analyzed the data using three ordered steps: (a) I set apart and codified portions of my data into emergent themes. My entire data set included audiotaped transcriptions, emails from parents, letters written to teachers from parents, and researcher's journals. (b) I highlighted each theme using Microsoft software automatic color scheme. This systematized coloring allowed me to organize my data. For example, when I repeatedly saw that someone made reference to enjoying the curriculum of in-home, one-on-one tutoring, I titled this theme "Enjoys Tutoring (ET)." I then sub-coded the theme within parentheses "student likes curriculum" and highlighted it bright green. (c) I placed the themes alphabetically into tables in order to make them accessible for further analysis (See Table 1 for a sample and Appendix E for the complete set of Data Analysis Tables).

Protection of Human Subjects

Prior to the implementation of this study and the approval from the University of San Francisco's IRBPHS committee, I wrote and distributed a letter to students who receive this tutoring. This letter explained clearly both the problem and the purpose statement of this study to the parents and the participants.

In addition, this letter discussed the specifics and the step-by-step process of the study. Furthermore, the research process and questions were fully disclosed to the students and parents in this letter. Neither the participants nor the parents were harmed in any way, and the interviews were conducted strictly on a voluntary basis. Finally, this letter asked the parents' permission for their K-12 children to be interviewed (See Appendices A-D for IRBPHS forms).

Table 1
Color Coded Research Themes (Positive)

Theme	Participant/ Caregiver
PGCBT (Learned how to focus more)	Jerele's Mother
PGCBT (Improved overall effort)	Jamie's Grandmother, Jerele's Mother
PGCBT (Feels confidence has improved)	Dario's Mother, Jamie's Grandmother, Jerele, Jerele's Mother
PIHT (It's quiet and calm)	Jerele
PTAT (Both improve academics)	Jeremiah, Shareek

Note. ES = Enjoys School (Blue), GTCH = Good Teaching (Sky Blue), KAIS = Knowledge Acquired in School (Lime), ET = Enjoys Tutoring (Bright Green), GTTR = Good Tutoring (Dark Teal), KAIT = Knowledge Acquired in Tutoring (Plum), PGCBT = Personal Growth Caused By Tutoring (Lavender), PIHT = Prefers In-Home Tutoring (Blue-Gray), PTAT = Prefers Teaching and Tutoring (Sea Green).

Methodological Reflections

As this data collection process began, I was concerned that my research participants and their parents were not giving me the responses I needed. I likened their responses to kindergarteners because they were not as profound as I wanted them to be. At this point in my negative judgment, I began to analyze my own character flaw – I was the problem! I did not like the data collection process because it felt unauthentic. Many of the participants and their parents trusted me with their thoughts, feelings, and emotions. I felt uncomfortable peering into my personal journals and asking the participants to explain themselves as if they were on the witness stand. I wanted my participants to answer my Eurocentric questioning with details that would be able to capture their complete educational experience. Although I understood the necessity of this data collection process, I remained uncomfortable while collecting my data. I continuously asked myself whom this process benefited, and the only answer I could muster was "Me."

I felt this way because no matter how much data I gathered, coded, and analyzed, my participants' lives remained the same. Although they have been changed by the effort, determination, and care I put forth in my tutoring, many students remain impoverished, live in rundown projects, and experience inadequate education daily. This is a burden I cannot change, especially knowing my personal privileges. I have the choice to come home and live in an environment free of shootings in the vicinity, eat everyday without worry, and attend a school where I receive one-on-one personal attention from professors who genuinely care.

Therefore, my frustration with this data collection process was the lack of systemic change this process had on my research participants. I am able to receive a dissertation from this process, and my research participants receive nothing in return. Throughout this data collection process, I talked to my participants and their parents about my discomfort and thanked them consistently for being a part of my life. This is important to mention because I feel my work is not research but life search. In-home, one-on-one tutoring of African American males is a journey that has been essential in my life years before the dissertation and data collection process. Furthermore, this journey will continue to be fundamental in my life long after the dissertation and data collection process are completed.

Similar to Fine et al. (2006), I was aware of my own influence and how it played out in the tutor-tutee relationship. For example, because of our close relationship, the tutees could have sabotaged the interviews by being overly subjective about their experiences in public school and in-home, one-on-one tutoring, making the data dishonest. In fact, my participants answered every question comprehensively and truthfully. Additionally, I tried to make sure my students spoke their minds authentically during the interviews. I knew my participants for several years and we had built relationships in which they entrusted me with their personal issues. I hoped that this trust was carried out through the interviewing process. I also ensured authenticity through the triangulation process, including the parent dialogues from the researcher's journal and emails.

Freire (1992) claims true change evolves when individuals put into practice "praxis: reflection and action upon the world in order to transform it" (p. 33). This statement holds true for my methodology. My research may lead to modification of in-school and after-school programs involving African American males, especially in the area of teacher education. Furthermore, through this process of reflection during the interviews, the tutees might be able to transfer their critical knowledge to younger siblings or peers.

For me as a researcher I was able to enhance my critical consciousness through the students' perspectives on how to better educate African American males and how in-home, one-on-one tutoring can work together in partnership with public schools. In closing, I feel that this kind of interviewing process is very personal and sacred. It is a transformative process for both the researcher and the research participant. This process is similar to Freire's (1992) notion of true dialogue, which he contends comes from a place of love, humility, and faith.

CHAPTER IV

PROFILES

In order to comprehend the full scope of in-home, one-on-one tutoring, the researcher's background and the foundation and daily routine must be explained. After working with several Jackson, California, non-profit organizations and school districts as a teacher and tutor, I began to independently tutor students 15 years ago. For me, this experience has been phenomenal because I enjoy the personal environment of each student's home. In this chapter, I profile my personal background, the tutoring program, and the participants.

Researcher's Background

I believe my passion for tutoring African American males stems from my personal transition and growth caused by my grandmother and mother's positive role modeling of resilience. In this section, I discuss how my grandmother, Cora Reynolds, and my mother, Ursulanda Horn, modeled perseverance, hard work, and Black pride which shaped my identity as a Black man committed to his students. Their resilient spirits have helped me navigate through a society in which I constantly struggle to maintain a balance between being Black in mainstream America. Although I maintain a powerful love for my Black culture as I negotiate mainstream culture, I fear that Eurocentric American values may suppress my Black pride.

Pride in my Black culture stems from being raised as a strong Black male from the Delores Heights neighborhood of Jackson, California. In my community of Delores Heights, I am respected for my education. For example, whenever I return to Delores Heights and converse with old friends, people, whom I call my *hommies* or *potnas*, revere me as someone who made it, and they are proud of my success as an educated Black male.

It is the Black women in my family who have influenced me the most in attaining my strong Black male identity. For instance, my grandmother symbolizes perseverance and Black pride. She teaches that her pride in being Black has allowed her to persevere through the challenges she often endured growing up in a white-dominated society. Her life experience of perseverance as a Black woman had an unfathomable effect in the shaping of my strong Black identity. For example, while working for the Market Street railroad in Jackson, California, as a street car conductor during the 1940's, she was insulted on a daily basis with racial slurs and epithets. Any probing of my grandmother on how she survived the challenges of her employment would result in an exclamation "You just have to be proud of being Black."

My mother is the backbone of my immediate family (composed of my older brother and myself). As in many African American single-parent families, the woman retains the family structure. My mother became both my father and mother after my parents divorced. Throughout her stressful divorce and family preservation, she remained a strong Black woman. She too, like my grandmother, consistently modeled a behavior of hard work and Black pride. She always teaches me that you have to work hard in life, especially being Black in America. One powerful example that illustrates the effect my mother's work ethic and cultural pride had on my identity was how I survived throughout college.

During my freshman year of college, I was not in a position to concentrate exclusively on my studies due to a lack of finances. Because my Mom always modeled an incessant work ethic, I constantly kept a job in college while the majority of my white peers attended classes without any other responsibilities. During my midterms and final examinations, I was fatigued because I worked several jobs. Although my grades were not exceptional, I completed my Bachelor's degree and worked unrelentingly to obtain my Master's degree. My success is a direct result of my mother's cultural pride and work ethic. The behavior that she modeled to me as a child allowed me to survive economically and academically.

In summary, both my grandmother and my mother through their unrelenting perseverance, work ethic, and Black pride have shaped my identity as a strong Black male. I am forever thankful for what these two amazing Black women in my life have taught me. In turn I try to inspire the same sense of perseverance, strong work ethic, and Black pride among the African American males I tutor. My grandmother and mother's role modeling helped me become an effective teacher and tutor because they modeled resiliency. Therefore, I have a great passion and commitment for my work with African American males.

In-Home, One-on-One Tutoring

In-home, one-on-one tutoring involves a series of tasks which help minimize disorganization. Overall, the initial process of my in-home, one-on-one tutoring takes an average of five days to complete, beginning from the day a student is referred to me from the community through word-of-mouth until the day I start tutoring. This process involves a sequence of dialogues that allow parents and students sufficient time to familiarize themselves with in-home tutoring, and the tutor, as well as to talk candidly about their concerns and goals.

I find this process instrumental because I wholeheartedly believe in structure and organization. In my work with in-home tutoring, I have seen how structure and care enhance the academic performance of students. For that reason, I have developed an intake process that allows students to dialogue, review materials and outlines, and inquire about the tutorial methodology prior to the initiation of tutoring. Table 2 describes this intake process, which consists of the above coordination and set-up tasks.

Table 2

Process of In-Home, One-On-One Tutoring

Timetable	Task 1	Task 2	Task 3
Day 1	Referral	Phone Call	Schedule Meeting
Day 2	Parent Dialogue	Student Dialogue	Group Dialogue
Day 3	Analysis of Notes	Categorization Placement	Initiation of Tutoring
Day 4	Curriculum Delivery	Review of Guidelines	Inquiry Session
Day 5	Beginning of Tutoring	Parent Dialogue	Adjustment Session

Most of my tutoring occurs in the evening after parents have come home and settled down. I tutor every student two hours per week and charge $30.00 per hour. The students I tutor in Delores Heights are referred through family members and friends. After I talk with caregivers and the potential tutees together, I have one-on-one dialogues with them. The purpose of these dialogues is to gain understanding about the group and individual goals for tutoring. After taking detailed notes and gathering basic information, I recommend two types of tutoring: scheduled or floating.

Scheduled tutoring is for students who can commit to being tutored at a designated home space and consistent time for an entire school year, not including holidays and illnesses. Floating is for students who cannot commit to a chosen time or place for many reasons. Usually, this person does not want to dedicate himself right away. Regardless of the category, each type of student receives the same type of tutoring service. I believe my in-home, one-on-one tutoring provides stability amidst chaotic home environments, a structured intake process, a well-crafted tutorial homework portfolio, a caring relationship, and educational field trips. These factors, along with the support of family members and the community, make up the organization of my in-home, one-on-one tutoring.

After many years of observation, I found that a stable home environment, regardless of socioeconomic status, helps accomplish successful in-home, one-on-

one tutoring. Most tutees have stable environments but some do not. Many of the students, who come from what I consider stable home environments, have a caregiver that cooks them a meal consistently, identifies and maintains a study area within the home, and involves them in various types of after-school activities. Conversely, tutees from unstable environments have not been prepared meals, have no designated study area, and are not involved in any after-school activities.

Another central factor in my tutoring is the tutorial curriculum portfolio. All of my students receive a tutorial homework portfolio maintained in a three-inch black binder. The purpose of the portfolio is to enhance skills in life, math, reading and comprehension, vocabulary, spelling, and writing. Every month I engage in an art project using everyday materials to represent life as the students see it at that point in time. This project allows students to draw a picture of what they deem their current reality. Students are free to portray detail that describes their environment. This project appears to be effective because students are able to name or "codify," in Freire's (2005) words, their current reality as well as make future projections.

An additional feature of my in-home tutoring is the focus on dialogues with the tutees. During every tutoring session, I allow time for students to share their personal and educational battles they face in public school and the community. These sessions allow students to talk candidly about their experiences and to discuss any tension or stress during school that may prevent them from fully engaging and enjoying the tutorial experience. Many of the tutees have stories from school that are unpleasant or disturbing. This time allows them to discuss their feelings openly without fear of judgment. As an African American male, I believe that having these discussions helps my tutees connect positively with another African American male, develop their identity, and recognize the possibilities of survival in a Eurocentric society.

At the end of each month, I take all of my students on field trips to libraries, universities, and bookstores. Similar to caring relationships, fieldtrips help to facilitate dialogues that allow the students to voice their frustrations from assignments they may be struggling with both in school and tutoring. The tutees also discuss their recommendations for making tutoring more effective, including how to increase their understanding of a particular skill.

Participants

Here I profile the African American males who participated in my study. Although each has his own unique identity and cultural background, Dario, Jamie, Jerele, Jeremiah, Shane, Shareek, and Taylor share similar experiences of public school and in-home, one-on-one tutoring. Everyday one or more of my students endure neighborhood violence, inadequate education, and lack of Black male guidance. In my opinion, these young Black males are heroes. Table 3 provides a description of each participant at the time this study was conducted including their age, grades, academic gifts and barriers to education, and the total number of years of in-home, one-on-one tutoring. All students attend schools in Jackson Unified School District.

Table 3

Descriptive Profile of Research Participants

Pseudonym	Age	Grade	Gifts	Barriers	Tutored
Dario	11	Fourth	Debating	Dislikes Organization	2 yrs.
Jamie	14	Eighth	Humor	Dislikes Reading	1 yr.
Jerele	16	Ninth	Determination	Dislikes Math	4 yrs.
Jeremiah	14	Eighth	History	Dislikes Politics	1 yr.
Shane	13	Eighth	Dialogue	Dislikes Math	1 yr.
Shareek	17	Eleventh	Debating	Dislikes Organization	1 yr.
Taylor	11	Fifth	Memory	Dislikes Pedagogy	3 yrs.

Dario

Dario is an 11-year-old African American male from Delores Heights whom I have been tutoring for two years. He attends an elementary school. He is a vivacious, attentive, and inquisitive young man. He currently lives with his mother and two younger siblings in his grandmother's house in Delores Heights. He has a host of cousins, aunts, nieces, and nephews who also stay with his grandmother.

Dario is about four feet tall and growing. He has caramel-colored skin and keeps his hair short and tapered. His smile and face light the room when he walks into the presence of others. He usually wears baggy jeans and sports the latest version of *Nike* brand shoes. Dario has a bright smile and a small rounded shaped head, which makes him resemble his mother. When I close my eyes and dream about what African tribe he is from, the vision I usually receive is that of a proud South African tribe, possibly the Zulu Nation. Although I have never been to South Africa, his face reminds me of my South African friends. Their rounded faces and their pleasant smiles are representative of the beautiful men and women of South Africa. Dario's distinguished characteristics are his ability to debate and his enthusiastic spirit.

One of Dario's favorite subjects is automobiles. He often points to various cars as we drive down the road on our monthly field trip visiting libraries and universities. On one of our recent field trips to Borders bookstore, he shouted, "Oh, man see that car, I wan that one....Yeah, that's a 500 series Mercedes, Benz!" I was amazed at his knowledge of this particular type of car. He smiled at me as if he knew I was stunned. He has a keen knowledge of cars. While in the store, I noticed Dario peering toward the automobile section. All of a sudden, he sprinted to the section and shuffled through some books. I burst into laughter because I was adamant on showing him Black history books. While he read the various magazines and books on cars, he started yelling out various sizes, shapes, and manufacturers of automobiles. As he perused the different magazines and books, I watched in appreciation at the glimmer in his eyes (Researcher's Journal, April 8, 2008).

Another distinct feature about Dario is his ability to debate. When I first met him two years ago, he was quiet and reserved. As our tutorial relationship developed, he began opening up to me about everything. More specifically, he started to debate and question everything. In addition, Dario's spiritual characteristic is one of his greatest strengths. He has three partially amputated fingers on his left hand. When he was younger, he was injured in an accident that caused his finger tips to be cut off. When Dario talks about other children teasing him, he usually becomes frustrated. Regardless of his partial amputee, he is always cheerful in tutoring. His motivational energy allows us to engage in in-depth conversations about school and life in general. He attributes his spirit and enthusiasm to his belief in God.

On many nights, Dario and I have countless conversations about life. He is constantly referring to God and Jesus in all of our conversations about life. I enjoy seeing his face light up when he discusses his personal beliefs about Christianity. I often smile and listen as if I were receiving a sermon from one of my former Baptist preachers. Who knows, maybe he will become a preacher one day! Dario's gift of an inspirational spirit motivates me because I am amazed at his self-assurance at such a young age.

On the other hand, Dario often struggles with tutoring because of the environment where he lives. When we first began tutoring, he was living with his mother in Delores Heights where he learned to adjust to the occasional gunfire and violence. During his early years in Delores Heights, Dario found it difficult to complete homework that required his full concentration and attention. This was extremely hard to achieve under these stressful conditions. His mom informed me "...Man, they was breaking in our house...they was shootin' almost everyday and we had to bounce... I couldn't even live up there any more..." (Researcher's Journal, January 9, 2007).

During our initial tutoring sessions in Delores Heights, I encouraged him to stay organized and attentive during tutoring. We developed consistent study times to meet along with detailed study habits focused on vocabulary words. I worked exhaustively with Dario to practice his enunciation and spelling of vocabulary words. Dario and I worked laboriously until he was able to increase his vocabulary skills. When Dario moved in with his grandmother, we kept our same study habits. Dario's vocabulary continues to be one of his outstanding skills. Although his grandmother's house is located in a less violent area than his mother's house, Dario is still faced with drug dealing and occasional killings.

Recently, Dario and I discussed some of the barriers to studying at home. To understand these barriers, one must consider the context of Dario's living conditions. Although he has a safe environment with his grandmother, so many people are around that he often finds it difficult to study and concentrate. For example, when I visit Dario for tutoring, he often takes 15 to 20 minutes to be prepared. This includes gathering books, binders, writing utensils, and paper. The most frustrating task for Dario is keeping the kitchen table clean. The table is the center of all his family activities.

Dario and I often study at the table and sometimes find it unusable – dirty and soiled with trash. Dario struggles with cleaning it up because he feels it is not his job to clean up after his family. After observing his frustration, I talked to his mother, grandmother and other family members about the importance of having a study area. Since then, his grandmother acquired a study table for tutoring and a space for Dario's educational materials.

During one tutorial session, Dario talked about his improvements in tutoring. He exclaimed, "Aaron, I'm getting better huh? I have a place where I keep all my stuff and no body can touch it." Dario's improvement has affected our study time drastically. Due to the family's budgetary confinement, I am only allotted two hours per week, which we are able to use effectively due to his growing degree of organization (Researcher's Journal, December 4, 2007).

Jamie

Jamie is a 14-year-old African American male who attends a middle school in Jackson and whom I have tutored for one year. Jamie has lived in Delores Heights with his grandmother and uncle since he was a baby. As an infant, his mother was addicted to crack cocaine, and he was placed in his grandmother's care. Jamie adapted well to his grandmother despite his occasional challenges as a youth.

Jamie is five feet tall with light brown-colored skin and short thick black hair. He is slightly overweight due in part to his sugar diabetes. His arms are very long and his smile is electrifying, especially when he is blissful. For example, I remember on Valentine's Day this past February, he was elated about dating this young Filipina girl at his middle school. He asked me questions about dating, including the ideas he planned for the day. I was excited for him because he was smiling from one cheek to the other. His smile on that day was particularly memorable because it revealed an inner peace. In order to help ease his Valentine tension, I gave him a stuffed rose to give to his girlfriend. Jamie and I often talk about that experience as if it just occurred. I reminded him of the smile he flaunted on that day. I will always remember his Valentine's Day smile because it would have made the entire population of Jackson smile on that day if they saw his face (Researcher's Journal, February 13, 2008).

Jamie's distinctive characteristics are his sense of humor and ability to communicate. During tutoring, Jamie and I often laugh aloud because he has a unique way of observing the world. He often imitates teachers whom he dislikes and he impersonates people well. I remember talking to him about his experience at his former middle school. Jamie had informed me that teachers were teasing him about his inability to be a successful student. Although he was upset, he imitated one of the teachers who participated in this conversation. Even though I had never met this teacher, the way he mimicked her with such enthusiasm led me to laugh hysterically. A few months later, I attended a school meeting where this same teacher was talking. During her conversation, I could not help but snicker at Jamie's precise impersonation (Researcher's Journal, January 16, 2008).

I believe one of Jamie's most powerful gifts is his ability to dialogue. When I first met Jamie, he was shy and quiet. After getting to know me, he began to open up and converse about school and personal life. He loves to ask questions and opine about various personal and political issues. For instance, one night after tutoring ended, we started talking about politics. I was so amazed to hear his response about United States politicians running for president. Jamie explained to me, "Man, I'm voting for Obama…I ain't goin' to pass up this chance to vote for a Black man…Hillary Clinton, she cool, but for me as a Black man, I'm voting for another Black man. Who you votin' for Aaron?" (Researcher's Journal, February 5, 2008).

As I sat in my chair with my mouth ajar, I could not believe Jamie was discussing politics. I was in awe because he had never discussed politics during our history lessons. What took place for the next hour and a half was a magnificent conversation about politics, life, and education. During that evening, Jamie described why he felt the teachers in his elementary school were racist. He talked about Black children being kicked out of his elementary school because teachers were afraid of them. I admire Jamie's motivation to dialogue because I believe this skill has enhanced his academics in that he was able to express himself more in class dialogues (Researcher's Journal, February 5, 2008).

Similarly, during a tutorial session in 2007, Jamie talked about his brother who died when Jamie was young. When I asked him about this traumatic event, he exclaimed, "I loved him a lot and I miss him. It feels weird not having him around anymore." Jamie was very close to his brother. He has a picture of him on his grandmother's mantle next to his mother and other family members. Although he appears to have resolved his brother's death, his grandmother and mother believe many of his inappropriate school behaviors can be attributed to the death of his brother. Jamie and I have a trusting relationship that is evolving with each tutorial session. I appreciate his willingness to be vulnerable and discuss his beliefs about politics and his personal life (Researcher's Journal, December 5, 2007).

On the contrary, Jamie's major problem in school is his lack of reading skills. After my many inquiries, Jamie informed me that he does not like reading. He claims since childhood he has never liked reading because he feels reading is a waste of time and effort. Since our tutoring, his attitude toward reading has changed slightly. Although he has not been reading consistently, I consider his effort a victory. My purpose for Jamie's tutoring is to expose him to different types of literature, including poetry, Black culture, autobiographies, and travel, in order to inspire him to read more frequently.

Once a month, Jamie and I visit local libraries and bookstores. He enjoys browsing through different types of books. I remember our first visit in the spring of 2007 when we entered Borders bookstore near Jackson State University. As soon as we walked into the store, he was amazed by all of the books. He nervously talked about people who were in the store and how expensive things were as if he was trying to ease his own discomfort. As we walked around, I encouraged him to glance at titles, open pages, and read portions of books. He immediately gravitated towards the magazine section with wrestling and video games.

After he read a few magazines, I took him over to the dictionary and thesaurus section of the store to preview all of the recent Webster's dictionaries. I encouraged him to review different types of dictionaries so that he could choose one he felt comfortable using. After spending about an hour in the store, I asked Jamie to select a book that I would purchase for him. Surprisingly, he refused my offer but suggested he would do so on our next trip. Although Jamie did not purchase any books, this experience was rewarding for me because I was able to expose him to the bookstore. During the ride home, we discussed the relevance of books and how reading can enhance other academic skills. He laughed and said,

"Yeah, you right, I know I need to read more but I just don't like it because it's boring" (Researcher's Journal, February 7, 2007).

Jamie's conversation and feelings expressed on this particular day motivated me to read with him during every tutorial session. Since our visit to the bookstore, I have shared several literature pieces with him, reading a few pages myself and then having him read. We often laugh at words that seem difficult to pronounce. He really enjoys reading about Martin Luther King Jr. and Malcolm X. During the end of the Spring 2008 semester, we read about Shaka Zulu who was one of the most powerful Kings who ruled South Africa. Jamie enjoyed the discussion questions I prepared for this reading because he was able to utilize his conversation skills. He discussed how Shaka Zulu made his army fight faster and how he would have led the troops in battle as an African King. Despite his dislike for reading, I believe Jamie's ability to communicate has somewhat increased his interest.

Jerele

Jerele is a 16-year-old high school African American male who was born and raised in Delores Heights. I have known him his entire life and he is very special to me because of our lifelong relationship. I tutored Jerele periodically for 10 years, and now consistently since 2004. At birth, Jerele was left abandoned with a damaged liver caused by his birth mother's use of crack cocaine. As a result of his damaged liver, Jerele had several surgeries to repair his liver until he was able to have a liver transplant operation.

Since then, Jerele has had numerous surgeries which make his stomach look as if someone tried to murder him in cold blood with a blunt object. His stomach is lined with scar tissue that has healed over the years in rows of thick sinew. I remember when he was young; he was unable to speak articulately because of his open trachea. He often pointed to his scar tissue, shaking his head in disappointment. As Jerele aged, I could see him develop physically and mentally before my eyes. Because of the damage caused by the crack cocaine,

Jerele is developmentally delayed. In short, this means that his brain development is not representative of his actual age. Despite some periodic internal bleeding and bouts with asthma, doctors have nursed Jerele to good health.

Jerele has a slender build with coffee-colored skin, which always looks glossy and smooth. His eyes are dark brown with stark white eye balls, giving him an intense stare. He has long eyelashes that you can see flutter from miles away when he continually closes and opens his eyes. His braces make his smile warm and inviting, and he speaks in a raspy voice because of the open trachea he had for years as a child. Jerele is fond of computer games and hip hop culture, but his most noticeable characteristics are his zeal for life and his enjoyment of speaking Ebonics among his friends.

Despite his health issues, Jerele is always excited and inspired about life, especially tutoring. Jerele demonstrates his enthusiasm at every tutorial session. Prior to tutoring, we frequently discuss his day as he joyfully expresses his excitement with my presence. He usually lunges toward me as I enter his home and gives me a big hug. As we make our way upstairs to the kitchen, Jerele sprints ahead of me yelling out to his mother about my being there. As we engage in tutoring, he often asks me about my day, especially my work with other students and my college experiences.

On one particular occasion, I remember Jerele getting his first 3.5 grade point average on his report card in middle school. As soon as I arrived at his house, he swung open the door and exclaimed, "Hey Aaron, you hear the good news...Yeah boy, yo boy doing Big Pimpin'!" Jerele's excitement was so rewarding to watch because he had been putting forth an extraordinary amount of effort throughout the semester. We worked arduously to increase all his grades and, as a result, our labor paid off. Jerele is an inspirational and competitive young man. In spite of all of his medical problems, his motivation has helped to improve his academics (Researcher's Journal, November 14, 2006).

On the contrary, Jerele's major issue in tutoring has been his dislike for math. Since I can remember, Jerele has always had a discontent for math. In elementary and middle school, he felt teachers did not explain math well. He enjoys doing math with me because he feels I am patient with him. An example of this patience was demonstrated one evening this year as we discussed one of his homework assignments regarding equations. I explained to Jerele that the goal of solving equations is to isolate the variables represented in each equation.

I then proceeded to show him in a written step-by-step process in which I had him review, copy, and explain in his own words. Afterwards, he completed an entire assignment of solving equations with unknown variables with no further assistance. What was significant about this learning experience is that I realized Jerele was able to comprehend equations rapidly with prolonged one-on-one tutoring. Additionally, the quiet and unrushed pace of in-home, one-on-one tutoring allowed him the time and space to acquire the knowledge of solving equations on that particular evening. Regardless of his health, and his dislike for math, Jerele's motivation continues to improve his academics.

Jeremiah

Jeremiah is a 14-year-old African American male middle school student whom I have tutored for one year. He lives with his mother and stepfather in Delores Heights with a whole host of brothers, sisters, uncles, and cousins. When he was a baby, his biological father was killed by gunshot. Although he has been exposed to violence throughout his childhood, his mother has consistently cared for him. Jeremiah is about five feet tall with a round-shaped figure. He walks as if he is limping and usually maintains a balance of indifferent and calm facial expressions. He is slightly overweight, frequently gasping for air as he talks. He walks lethargically as he lumbers about his business. His face is carved and dark brown. His eyes are slightly concaved within his head, resembling the face of a strong Nigerian male.

In the course of Jeremiah's violent neighborhood, he has maintained an interest in African American literature. By far, this is his most unique characteristic. He is extremely proud of being Black and enjoys the Afrocentric curricula I prepare within the homework portfolio that discuss the Kings and Queens that once ruled Africa as well as African American history. When I read Black history to Jeremiah, I can see his shoulders raise erect and his back straighten because of the sense of pride that immediately enters his spirit. For example, during one tutoring session last year, I was reading with him an article on proud African American fathers in the *Black Journal of Education*. As we read the article, I watched his eyebrows wrinkle in curiosity about the explanations given by the fathers who loved their children despite their personal hardships. When we discussed the relevance of the article, Jeremiah was candid about the different African American males in his life, especially a teacher at his middle school named Mr. Clayton.

He spoke about how Mr. Clayton takes the African American boys from his middle school to different presentations in Jackson that help young Black men stay out of trouble. In particular, he mentioned a field trip with Mr. Clayton to the Jackson Boys Club. He was excited about the different Afrocentric topics they discussed throughout the night. Jeremiah compared Mr. Clayton's characteristics with the Black men in the article we read. This experience allowed me to observe Jeremiah's passion for African American literature through his outspoken dialogue, which has in a roundabout way led to an increased interest in his education.

In contrast with his enjoyment for African American literature, Jeremiah has experienced inadequate education in the JUSD. For instance, he was suspended from his middle school for what he called a minor incident that occurred between him and another student. His suspension lasted for two days and Jeremiah was extremely upset. He informed me that he disliked the white counselor who suspended him because as he stated "she always be suspending the Black kids for no reason" (Researcher's Journal, November 9, 2007).

After listening to Jeremiah voice his frustration about this particular counselor, I was able to engage in a dialogue with him about the topic of racism and the education of African American males within the United States. As we talked about these issues that are personal to both of us, I noticed that Jeremiah began to laugh and unwind during our discussion. He informed me later in the week that he was able to stay focused at school and to forget about the incident. He thanked me for listening and talking to him. In spite of this experience with racism, Jeremiah's love for African American literature has increased his interest in education.

Shane

Shane is a 13-year-old African American male middle school student whom I have tutored for a year. He lives with his two fathers in Delores Heights. He was born in New York, but has lived the greater part of his life in Jackson, California. When he was a baby, his father Gavin adopted him. He was found in his diapers in a crack house that his birth mother, addicted to crack cocaine, had been using for refuge and drug binges.

Shane is five feet tall with dark tan skin and a gleaming smile. He always sports a pair of jeans with a baseball cap tilted to the side, looking like the famous rapper, Jay Z, from New York. He talks very slowly and calmly as if he methodically thinks about every single word he uses. He is as cool as still water on a winter night. When we tutor, he leans back in his chair as if he were driving a '57 low rider Chevy Malibu. He talks as if he has an old soul, constantly peering into your eyes trying to hypnotize you into a deep sleep. In other words, this young man epitomizes the word "cool."

By looking at Shane and his coolness, you couldn't tell he was left in his diapers in a crack house. He loves wrestling and conversation. He often discusses his wrestling talent with me during tutoring. He gets energized talking about slamming other kids in wrestling practice. He always inquires about specific techniques for handling larger boys. For example, during one tutoring session he asked me how to slam someone that he was having difficulty wrestling at practice. I talked about using the strength of his legs and hips when slamming someone. We discussed my wrestling experience in the military where I was trained in Gracie jiujutsu – a specialized style of wrestling. He was so engaged that he wanted to practice right there in the coffee shop where we were studying.

In addition to his passion for wrestling, Shane loves to dialogue. We often communicate about a range of topics in the Black community. On one particular tutoring session, Shane asked me about the word "Nigger" and how many urban males use it casually every day. He was confused about using this word with his friends because he believed it was inappropriate. His thoughts were articulate and concise. He expressed that when Black boys use the word in public, society becomes unaffected by the harmful meaning of the word. Furthermore, he articulated that Black people should not use this word because it allows others to think of Black people derogatively. As I listened to Shane express himself, I was impressed by his ability to get straight to the point. This experience helped me realized how Shane's ability to converse will allow him to debate the most influential subjects within the Back community and the larger society.

Shane often struggles with boredom in school. Although he takes responsibility for his faults in school, he believes that school is boring. After talking to him throughout the school year, Shane discussed that he is bored with school because of the insignificant work his teachers assign daily. He expressed that many of his teachers often dispense ambiguous dittoes and homework that he feels are unrelated to life. These assignments only increase his boredom. Consequently, he often leaves class in frustration.

Moreover, Shane dislikes math. He often neglects to study his multiplication tables, refuses to practice for his math tests, and purposefully neglects his math homework. His dislike for math started in middle school because he felt teachers didn't seem to care about the assignments. For the past year, I have worked laboriously with Shane to lessen his apprehension for multiplication but he still seems uninterested. Although he put forth a tremendous effort on the number of problems and assignments I created for him, he has remained disinterested in multiplication.

Although Shane struggles in school with boredom and math, he never gives me any problems in tutoring. I enjoy his passion for wrestling and conversation because they give him personality and confidence. His passion for conversation allows him to discuss important topics that may potentially affect the larger society. Therefore, I will continue to harness his ability to dialogue in an effort to allow Shane to be an outspoken high school student, college student, and citizen.

Shareek

Shareek is a 17-year-old African American male from Delores Heights. I have tutored Shareek for one year. Like my other students, Shareek was withdrawn when I first met him. At an early age, he lost his brother to a violent death; since then he has been too despondent to discuss what actually occurred. He has another older brother and sister who live with him. Shareek is about five feet seven inches tall, with a sleek, well-trimmed physique attributable to his consistent working out with weights in his basement at home. He often flares his muscles for me before tutoring. He often states, "Aaron, check this out, I got my swoll on, huh?" I enjoy listening to Shareek's reference to his muscles because they have a positive effect on his self-esteem. Shareek has short hair that used to be long and kept in a ponytail. Shareek's shiny light brown skin bares a resemblance to Malcolm X's face. Recently, Shareek sports a tiny mustache that he often grows into a goatee (Researcher's Journal, April 9, 2008).

What's more, Shareek is passionate about art and hip-hop music. We often talk about the latest rap album. For the most part, he is interested in college, has a passion for art, and makes an effort to communicate explicitly. Shareek loves to converse about college. He becomes excited when talking about learning new things and being on the college campus with the other students. He asks lots of questions about college. When he explains what college he wants to attend, you can sense the hesitancy in his voice about the environment of college. On many field trips, I frequently take Shareek to colleges I attended in Jackson as a means to expose him to the possibility of higher education.

During a recent visit to Jackson State University, I showed him around the entire campus, including the library, computer rooms, and financial aid office. Throughout our tour, he showed his excitement on his face. I introduced him to colleagues and former professors. He asked lots of questions about required classes by the University and study habits of a successful student. I believe this field trip gave him a realistic depiction of the college environment. Shareek's desire to attend college has improved his study habits in tutoring. I notice that he is more excited about learning how to read and frequently practices independently.

In addition to his interest in college, Shareek is a gifted artist. During tutoring, we regularly discuss art, including putting together his personal art portfolio. I encourage him to keep a detailed art portfolio that he can use in his professional career or when he decides to go to college. He is interested in attending college to study art. He is very gifted in the area of pencil sketching. He has a number of sketches that he keeps in a leather binder. His sketches are realistic in how they depict everyday life.

Furthermore, Shareek's ability to be candid over the past year has also been helpful in tutoring. On many occasions he talks about his embarrassment over his inability to read fluently. His honesty reflects a major improvement, because in the past Shareek would not discuss anything in tutoring. When I first met Shareek a year ago, he sat quietly in tutoring while I discussed the readings and other assignments. After a couple of months, he began opening up about his personal life, including his struggles with school. His candidness has led to more engaging tutorial sessions because I am now able to help Shareek with his academic limits without him feeling ashamed or guilty.

Taylor

Taylor is an 11-year-old African American male, born and raised in Delores Heights, who attends a local elementary school in Jackson. He currently lives with his two younger brothers in Delores Heights with his Uncle Jake and Aunt Vivica who adopted them recently. When he was young, his mother was on drugs and his father imprisoned. Because of Taylor's mother's inability to become clean and sober, the courts authorized his uncle and aunt to have full custody of Taylor and his brothers. I have tutored Taylor for three years and have come to enjoy every single minute of our tutoring.

Taylor is about four feet six inches with long arms and a muscular frame. He has honey brown skin with light brown eyes. His smile is bright and exudes confidence. He has short wavy hair which he grows out from time to time into a short thick Afro, resembling the one Jessie Jackson used to sport in his earlier years as a civil rights activist. His fingers are long and elegant with well-trimmed finger nails. He often wears jeans and a t-shirt to tutoring. Occasionally, he will have designer outfits that he loves to show off during tutoring. What I enjoy most about Taylor is his incredible memory and enthusiasm demonstrated in tutoring.

Taylor has an incredible memory. He is able to remember past and future appointments, things that people have said, and meals that he ate over the past months. I am amazed to listen to him recall some of the most random pieces of information. An example of his strong memorization skills occurred in 2006 during the fall. Taylor was talking about a meal that his aunt prepared and his face lit up as he discussed every single detail. He stated, "Man, Auntie Vivica cooked some screamin' chicken and greens! I ate all of my food!" His attention to detail is flawless. He was able to remember everything that his aunt prepared that evening, including the events that led up to the dinner (Researcher's Journal, October 3, 2006).

Taylor's ability to recollect information has also been beneficial to tutoring. On many occasions, Taylor and I complete tutoring in the middle of a unit plan I prepared for him. During subsequent tutorials, I usually begin with a "check-in and review" to inquire about the knowledge he retained from previous sessions. Amazingly, he is able to remember almost everything we discussed from our preceding tutoring, including the exact place within the unit we ended. Recently, his uncle mentioned that Taylor had received outstanding scores on his reading comprehension. In addition, his standardized test score in reading was improved. He thanked me for tutoring him, but I attribute his recent improvement in school and testing to his remarkable memory.

Taylor's enthusiasm for tutoring is unparalleled. He is always excited about reading and engaging in the different lesson plans I prepare for him. I tutor Taylor twice a week and our tutorials are intense. During every tutorial session, I read aloud and practice writing and vocabulary with Taylor. He enjoys reading books because he consistently asks to read aloud from his book selection during the reading component of tutoring. He is excited about the lesson plans which allow him to demonstrate his enthusiasm.

Case in point, one of the most enjoyable lesson plans that I worked on with Taylor was a human rights lesson which included the Universal Declaration of Human Rights (UDHR). During this lesson, I informed Taylor about the educational rights that were taken away from Blacks during and after slavery. We discussed the right to education, as predetermined in the UDHR, and how it is important to obtain an education which has not always been given to Blacks. For over a week, I talked with Taylor about how Martin Luther King Jr. and others who helped bring about justice and equality to many human beings, not just Black people. I also informed Taylor that Dr. King was an important person to the civil rights cause because he helped promote the practice of inadequate education as a global issue.

Taylor exhibited his understanding of human rights and Dr. King in a short video presentation about Martin Luther King, Jr. Taylor was thrilled during the entire presentation while presenting his information in a confident and professional manner. I admire Taylor's enthusiasm with tutoring because he is always prepared for tutoring and eager to learn. Although he continues to struggle with reading, in-home, one-on-one tutoring has been able to increase his love for reading by consistent practice and exposure to book stores and libraries (Researcher's Journal, March 27, 2007).

On the other hand, Taylor has had some difficulty in school. My observations of Taylor occurred periodically within his middle school classrooms. During these classes, Taylor has been passive at times because of the lack of appropriate pedagogical techniques which, without a doubt, has caused his reading skills to diminish. For example, during one of my visits to Taylor's classroom, I observed Taylor playing an unrelated computer game. After inquiring about this observation, the teacher informed me that this was a technique that he used for those deemed as "good students."

I was infuriated by the lack of care in Taylor's teacher. In order for Taylor to develop his learning potential, this teacher should have used Taylor's extra instructional time to practice reading. After conducting a meeting about Taylor's Individualized Educational Plan (I.E.P.), the members of his I.E.P. team were informed of this teacher's mediocre action. Since this meeting, the school has done nothing to either improve the teacher's training or support Taylor. This lack of effort from Taylor's school staff demonstrates a lack of care for providing him adequate education (Researcher's Journal, September 12, 2006).

In addition, his teachers' lack of involvement has had a negative effect on both Taylor and his Uncle Jake. His uncle informed me that he has also observed Taylor's teachers performing minimally during class. On many of his school visits, Uncle Jake observed the teachers placing Taylor on the computer after completing a simple kindergarten assignment – an assignment far below Taylor's capabilities. His uncle informed the teachers that he wanted them to challenge Taylor with reading assignments that would develop his reading skills, but the teachers informed Uncle Jake they do not have the appropriate resources. Although Taylor has experienced inadequate education, I believe his memory and enthusiasm have improved his learning.

In conclusion, every day I feel honored to work with my students because of their unique personality traits. The strengths shown during in-home, one-on-one tutoring enhance their academic experience.

CHAPTER V

FINDINGS

In this chapter I present an overview of the findings. Based on the broad generative themes that emerged from my entire data set, I address each component of my research questions separately with what I have categorized as satisfactory and unsatisfactory perceptions of school and in-home, one-on-one tutoring experiences. Under each of these categories, I present sub-themes that emerged from most of the data. Throughout my summaries, I use samples of raw data that include participants' and parents' responses to illustrate the findings.

Overview of Findings

In the following sections, I present the main findings and generative themes for each research question. While reviewing my entire data set, a number of significant broad generative themes emerged regarding the relationship and academic experiences of African American males in public school and in-home, one-on-one tutoring. For this chapter, I chose the themes that had the most graphic details. Not all of these themes are included in this chapter. For a complete list of themes and codes, please refer to Data Analysis Tables in Appendix E.

In general, the students and their parents held more negative than positive perceptions of public school. In contrast, the students and their parents had more positive than negative perceptions of in-home, one-on-one tutoring. Below is each research question with satisfactory and unsatisfactory perceptions about public school and in-home, one-on-one tutoring.

Research Question #1:

What Are the Teacher-Student Relationships and

Academic Experiences of African American Males in a Public School Setting?

Satisfactory Perceptions of Teacher-Student Relationships

Four participants said that some teachers encouraged students in public school. Shane and Jerele had the clearest point of view about teacher encouragement. Shane talked about the encouragement from his science teachers and administrators:

> A: How do the teachers demonstrate what they want you to do in school?

> S: Um, my science teacher, she always talks about me, well all my teachers, the principal, they always be saying I'm a bright kid and stuff. They need me to start doing your work (lowers his voice) and we want you to all go to college and have a good life, so, maybe that's it. (Interview with Shane, Wednesday, June 4, 2008).

Similarly, Jerele discusses his experiences with encouraging teachers:

> A: How do you feel your teacher wants you to do in school?

> J: I feel my teacher wants me to do well and (pauses) and be very and be on top of my work.

> A: And how do you know that?

> J: Because she gives me a, she gives me, (pauses) she, she gives me encouragement so I can stay focused.

> A: Can you talk about what type of encouragement, what type of things do they say?

> J: They say "good job," "keep going," they give me a high-five sometimes? (Interview with Jerele, Monday, June 2, 2008).

Jerele's opinion about encouragement illuminated how care was manifested by his ability to stay focused.

Satisfactory Perceptions of Public School Academic Experiences

Three participants enjoyed their academic experience when teachers helped them with homework. Dario conversed about his teachers:

A: And how do you feel about your teachers?

D: Um, I think they, I, I think they, I, I um, I think they good, they're good teachers and they help me learn. They help me with my homework and stuff. They help me learn a lot. That's why I feel good about them. And yeah, that's why. (Inaudible) They're a good teacher (Interview with Dario, Tuesday, June 3, 2008).

Likewise, Jerele discussed a specific teacher who helped him in school:

A: How do you feel about your teachers?

J: I feel like my teachers helped me, has helped me a lot. They help me when I had a problem with a question. They will sit down and talk about it.

A: And what makes you feel that way? Can you give an example?

J: I feel uh Ms. Manbahs likes to help me by going over stuff I don't understand or I am having trouble with and she corrects some of my homework I, I get wrong (swallows and pauses). (Interview with Jerele, Monday, June 2, 2008).

In both examples, Dario and Jerele divulged that teachers helped them comprehend assignments gave them positive impressions about their teachers.

Unsatisfactory Perceptions of Teacher-Student Relationships

Teachers Yelled at Students

Three participants shared that teachers yelled at students. During an interview, Dario expressed his experience with a teacher yelling:

D: His name is Mr. Retlaw and he yells at me when I'm just asking for work. He just say do your work (voice raises) and stuff. And I just ask for, ask for help. And he just help other people when I ask for help first.

A: How did that make you feel?

D: Not good, makes me want to like, yell at, makes me like want to yell at him and stuff but I don't because I know I was gone get in trouble, yell at him back. (Interview with Dario, Tuesday, June 3, 2008).

Dario's mother confirmed his story in a conversation about school, as shown in this account from my research journal:

Dario's mom and I talked about his classroom teacher. She informed me that she dislikes the school principal and the teachers. She feels the principal does not treat the Black parents fairly. She also feels that Dario's teacher does not know how to teach. She told me, "Mr. Retlaw (Dario's Teacher) can not teach Aaron, dude is a trip...his classroom is always out of control when I visit Dario." She believes Mr. Retlaw yells at Dario in class because he does not know how to control Dario (Researcher's Journal, April 4, 2006).

In Dario's experience, both he and his mother conveyed dislike toward Mr. Retlaw. I found Dario's mother's statement about Mr. Retlaw profound because she perceived his yelling as a lack of classroom management. This comment helped confirm that yelling was an ineffective classroom management tool for Dario. Similarly, Shareek discussed his experience with a teacher who yelled:

S: And then like, Uh, when I went to uh off to middle school this white teacher, he was trying to yell at me, and I yelled at him back. And I guess he got scared and (inaudible) I don't know, I was always getting into fights with him, you know, cuz I don't know, maybe he thought, I don't know, because I was Black or something, I don't know what it was, but yeah (Interview with Shareek, Wednesday, June 4, 2008).

Within Shareek's commentary, he used race to describe teachers yelling. His thoughts highlight the concept of systemic racism that exists among teachers in his public school experience, namely JUSD. Shareek's mother validated his story in a conversation about his public school experience in JUSD:

...I was appalled to hear yet another story of a teacher shouting at students from a parent's perspective. Ms. Harris told me, "A white teacher in Shareek's elementary school...she was treating the black kids wrong Mr. Horn...when they (Black kids) did something, she scold them okay...and when the white kids did something wrong, she didn't do anything...she used to always scream and yell at them Black kids fa no reason...you hear me...no reason..."

She stated that she had to constantly check on Shareek and his older bother when they attended Hanview Elementary School. She said,

"It was this Black teacher who I had to put in check at Shareek and dem elementary school...she was talking about them kids and hitting on them kids...one day Shareek was telling me that she was hitting on them kids and calling them names...(expletive)...yelling and hollering...I went to the principal and talked to him about this teacher who was hitting them kids...I told the teacher if she ever hit my kids, Imma beat her (expletive)…(I started laughing)…but the principal…he eventually fired her…"

In the same way, Shareek's mother emphasized the problem of systemic racism from her perspective. She felt this particular Black teacher treated the White kids more fairly than the Black kids. Ms. Harris expressed further thoughts about public school:

> …As we talked about improving the JUSD, she discussed, "it's horrible…I think they need cameras in the class… (expletive)…I used to come and pop in on Shareek unannounced so I can see his teachers on the spot…I think that half of them don't need to be teaching because they don't care…I'm telling you Mr. Horn, they need to be put cameras in the classroom…" It was good to sit down and talk to Ms. Harris. We had been talking on the phone for several weeks but today's conversation was refreshing because I finally got to hear her opinion on Shareek's experience with JUSD… (Researcher's Journal, August 15, 2007).

Most importantly, Ms. Harris felt that continual parent advocacy helped ease some of the inefficiency her sons experienced in public school. This type of parent support, exhibited by Ms. Harris, is one example of how systemic racism can be acknowledged and lessened in pubic schools.

Teachers Demonstrated Racism

Five participants articulated that teachers demonstrated racism toward African American male students in public school. During an interview with Jamie, we talked about his experience with a Chinese teacher he believed was racist:

> A: Okay and there was another experience that you had told me before about a teacher at Rainview Elementary. I think you said that she didn't want you being around because she was afraid of you. Can you talk about that experience?
>
> J: Because she was a short Chinese lady and no offense but Chinese really don't like Blacks and I'll, and I'm a tall Black kid and she didn't really like me.
>
> A: And can you, can you talk about that. How do you know that she didn't like you? What were some of the things that she did that showed you that she didn't like you?

J: Cause when I walked to her and tried to get some help she'll kind of step back and then step back around the desk so if I was trying to attack her I got to go around the desk. And when I would try to talk to her she'll walk a little faster so I have to run and catch her to ask her something.

A: And how does that make you feel when that happens?

J: It feels bad because I'm not trying to hurt the lady, I'm just trying to get an answer for my work.

A: And did your mom or your grandmother or anybody come down to talk to her or to, to talk about that situation?

J: Yeah they did and that's when they said I'm, I'm afraid of Jamie because he's a tall African American kid (Interview with Jamie, Thursday, June 5, 2008).

Jamie's experience was telling in that, akin to Shareek, he noted the race of his teacher as he described his experience. His comments brought forth the importance of how not talking about race influenced the people involved in public schooling, specifically the children. Jamie's teacher was wrong for practicing such discriminatory beliefs about Blacks. Jamie was wrong for using this experience to make a broad sweeping generalization about the entire Chinese race. Jamie's experience was authenticated by his grandmother in our conversation one evening about his JUSD experiences:

...At the end of the month, his grandmother talked to me about Jamie's past with Jackson Unified School District (JUSD). She talked about how he was always being suspended from elementary school. She said, "I don't think them teachers liked Jamie from da get go baby...this one Chinese lady used to always keep Jamie out in the hallway when it was cold...you know...I didn't appreciate that at all." She further informed me that Jamie's elementary teachers were afraid of him. She stated "Baby, that Chinese woman stood up and told me and Jamie's moma that she thought Jamie was getting to be too big for an African American student...you hear me Aaron...she did not want Jamie in her class anymore because she was afraid of him." Although I didn't' find it hard to believe the blatant racism from Jamie's teachers, I still found it hard to comprehend how this woman could be so callous towards Jamie and still be allowed to teach... (Researcher's Journal, December 5, 2007).

Jamie's grandmother's story was powerful because she disclosed parallel thoughts about this same teacher. His grandmother's remarks explained the audacity of this teacher's statement, generalizing that Black children should be feared when they reach a certain height.

In all of Jamie's experiences with this teacher, nothing compared to the inhumane treatment illustrated in the example below:

> A: I noticed you mentioned about a teacher putting you in the closet. Can you talk a little more about that in terms of you know describe what would make a teacher put you in the closet?
>
> J: It wasn't just me it was everybody. But why would you put a student in the closet for not just listening to you? That don't make sense. And it was rats in the closet too.
>
> A: And what were some of the things that caused this person to put you in the closet?
>
> J: Like I would be talking to another student when she trying to teach and then she would just put me in the closet. Or another student trying to talk to me and she'll put them in the closet.
>
> A: And how long did she keep you in the closet for?
>
> J: Until lunch or recess.

This sickening experience demonstrated the distorted power some teachers felt they had in public schools. This teacher's misuse of power and authority set the foundation for the vicious style of punishment used on Jamie and his peers. Jamie described more of his mistreatment:

> A: And did you have to sit, stand or, what, what did you do while you were in the closet as punishment?
>
> J: She had a desk already in there so whoever act up had a desk to sit there. You sit. And if it was two people, she would put two people. If it three people, she would put three people.
>
> A: And what was the name and, and nationality and, and gender this teacher?
>
> J: Chinese

A: And she was uh female or male?

J: Female

A: Umkay, and did your mom or you or anybody sit down and talk with this woman to, to talk about this experience?

J: Yeah, but she just said that I do it to all of the students not just him.

A: And what, what ever happen to that, that situation. Did she continue to put children in the closet?

J: She continued to put them in the closet but not me. Cause there, their parents never came but mine did.

A: And, and what do you think about that experience, uh after looking back on that. What does that all that make you think about.

J: That don't make sense putting a student in the closet just because he was talking. You can just, oh just listen but putting him in the closet with rats. That's just like torture. (Interview with Jamie, Thursday, June 5, 2008).

Jamie's experience was appalling, and his teacher should have been fired. Her inhumane tactics were as Jamie called them - torture. This case clearly called attention to the need to revamp JUSD, including the retraining of all administrators and teachers. JUSD should be informed about these types of incidents and they should address this particular type of inadequate education during teacher training.

In an interview with Jeremiah, he disclosed his thoughts about a teacher named Ms. Healy whom he alleged to be racist:

A: What was it about Ms. Healy? I know you mentioned her earlier before. You said she was racist. You said that she hated all the Black kids. Can you talk about that? Why did you think she hated all the Black kids? How did she treat the Black kids compared to all the other kids?

J: Whelp, I think that she's racist because she treats all the Black kids... she yells at 'em and if a like a Chinese person or another race person walk up to her, she uh act all nice but if a Black person walk up to her face, she tell 'em that something going on...she start yelling at 'em and want to call they mom and want to send 'em home and that's why I don't like her and that's why she racist!

A: Can you give me your definition of what you think racism is?

J: Like she, like we was in the uh gymnasium and we uh was, we was uh, we was getting' our cap and gowns and she, I was up there signing my papers and she was like Jeremiah if you don't sit down I'll suspend you and then I had barged outta there because she was saying she was going to suspend me for no reason (sniffles).

A: And what is your definition of racism, like your definition?

J: My definition of racism is that she (Ms. Healy) don't like Black kids and she don't, and she just like other uh kids and but if, if a Chinese person call us racist, she don't believe us, she gotta go to hecka people to ask 'em, like hecka witnesses and stuff. Why she just can't believe a Black person when they first say it?

It was interesting to hear Jeremiah's response about Ms. Healy because the more I tried to get him to establish a definition of racism, the more he discussed adamantly that Ms. Healy was racist. I continued to probe him about racism:

A: So it sounds like are you saying when someone is racist, that they hate other races?

J: Yeah, and then when we go up to tell her, she don't care about us. But if a person, like if a Chinese person come up to her and tell her that we was calling her Chinese and stuff then she a uh, try to suspend every last one of us for like five days or so.

A: And have you talked to her about your feelings about why you think she's racist or have your, have your mom or any of your family members talked to her about this uh, you know these issues of being suspended and her dealing with the Black kids a certain way?

J: No, not yet but imma have my mom (inaudible) try probably talk to her, probably tomorrow or so, but yeah she, my mom really do need to talk to her about that (Interview with Jeremiah, Friday, June 6, 2008).

Jeremiah's thoughts portrayed Ms. Healy's attitude that Chinese kids should be treated better than Black kids. Jeremiah's mother verified Ms. Healy's behavior in a conversation about Jeremiah's dislike for her:

"...everyone else want him to fail...especially that lady...Ms. Healy...I think she is racist...She cain't stand Jeremiah...It seem like she got it in for him...It's like she fixed on Jeremiah and the other Black kids...every time Jeremiah do one little thing Mr. Horn, here she come...she don't like Jeremiah at all and she especially don't like them Black kids...It's a trip cause she was one of my daughters teachers too...and she still da same after all these years..." (Researcher's Journal, January 18, 2008).

Ms. Verelle's opinion about Ms. Healy gave additional support for the systemic racism in JUSD, but also denoted the generational transference and practice of racism by a public school teacher, observed annually by Jeremiah's mom.

Teachers Did Not Care About Students

Three participants believed that teachers do not care. In my interview with Jeremiah, he described uncaring teachers in his middle school:

A: Can you talk about the teachers that you said don't care about you?

J: Whelp, like I said before, they don't care about me, cause they don't, they don't help me do nothing in class, if I raise my hand, she'll ask me to ask somebody else to help me do my work and then she'll go on and help somebody else instead of me (Interview with Jeremiah, Friday, June 6, 2008).

Jeremiah's description outlined the lack of accountability inherent in this teacher's display of not caring. Shareek discussed a similar experience:

A: So in the old school, you say your teachers didn't care

S: They did not care

A: Can you give an example of how they demonstrated them not caring?

S: I mean, like sometimes they may say like uh, (smacks teeth) like oh, like, like cuz some teachers would say uh you don't need that much credits right to get that, but basically you do though. And like sometimes they like say oh, like don't take that class when you really gotta take that class. They be saying unnecessary stuff, Like, like stuff that (inaudible) but why you, but why would you even say that, like don't take p.e. when you do gotta take p.e. (Interview with Shareek, Wednesday, June 4, 2008).

Shareek's account portrayed the lack of knowledge and professionalism intrinsic in this teacher's demonstration of not caring. Shareek furthered his definition of teachers not caring by describing a teacher who would fall asleep in class:

A: I remember you talking about, your teacher falling asleep in class, and can you tell me a little bit about that, like what used to happen and how'd that make you feel?

S: Man, he used to fall asleep like mostly everyday, and it showed to me like he didn't care. He was only there for the money. And it was like, it was like dam. He really like just, was just snoring in class. People was making fun of him. Like, man it was just, it was just terrible, just horrible. It was like; he was just coming there, just falling asleep. He wasn't teaching us. I mean he was giving us some packet work and just let us do it.

A: And did you or the other students try to complain or do anything?

S: Na, they didn't care either. They was like oh whatever like, he go to sleep, you know, (inaudible) I don't think they care; they didn't like they care. I mean some people asked for him to explain the work better. But he didn't explain the work better so they just asked uh the Black lady there so yeah, and then she just explained the work good and we just did it. You know. So it was all, it was all good (Interview with Shareek, Wednesday, June 4, 2008).

Shareek's narrative illustrated his perception of this teacher's blatant disrespect toward students. Remarkably, Shareek seemed impassive by this lack of care. In the same way, he described how students in this class eventually became uninterested in this teacher's lack of care. As a result, students modeled the same behavior. Taylor's uncle talked about why he felt Taylor's teachers did not care:

I talked to Uncle Jake about Taylor's issues with his schoolteacher, Mr. Ancelman. He told me that he feels Mr. Ancelman was not strict enough with Taylor. He said, "That man cain't teach...he worse than Taylor's other school teachers...I don't know Aaron...he don't wanna teach Taylor...like he don't care...every time I go down there, he always got Taylor up on the computer or somethin' like dat...He getting me frustrated.... He just don't care...you should see some of the other Black children in his class...they be running all over da place Aaron...he ain't got no control over them kids..." After Uncle Jake expressed his belief about Taylor's teacher, I started thinking about the parents of my other students who had spoken the same thoughts about their son's teachers (Researcher's Journal, December 5, 2006).

Uncle Jake's view of Mr. Ancelman is graphic because he gave a clear portrayal of not caring.

Unsatisfactory Perceptions of Public School Academic Experiences

Teachers Did Not Communicate With Parents

Three parents of the participants stated that teachers did not communicate with them. Dario's grandmother spoke about teachers who failed to communicate:

> ...She informed me, "I think he got the wrong end of the stick...he did not get the services that he needed Aaron...he was robbed of the proper services...Elaine Elementary dogged him out...the teachers did not communicate with me at all...they should have done a better job at that...it was always an open door policy with me but they never called Aaron...they never called me...I guess they was scared of me you know...them teachers did not like to see me come up there...you know...it was a mess at Elaine...they never called me unless it was something bad happening to Dario and the other boys (Her other grandchildren)..." (Researcher's Journal, March 25, 2008).

Dario's grandmother described how teachers opted not to call her because of what she described as fear. In a letter to JUSD, Shane's father addressed a teacher about her lack of communication:

> Gavin Martinson
> xxxxx Avenue
> Jackson, California xxxxx
> November 9th, 2005
>
> Dear Verma Meagan,
>
> It is very disconcerting to learn of this "serious difficulty" in your class, this late in the second report period. Given your refusal to utilize Shane's Student Planner as a forum to communicate with me, it's no wonder that his progress in your Science class has reached such a critical juncture. Had I been informed about this earlier in this report period, we may have been able to work together to assist Shane in finding ways to overcome the challenges he seems to be facing in your class.

In the beginning of Mr. Martinson's letter, he immediately addressed this teacher's lack of communication. Most noteworthy was that this teacher failed to communicate using a standardized system of communication created by JUSD and utilized throughout most mainstream classrooms. This failure to use a basic mode of communication showed disrespect for the student and the parents, but also for the school district. Mr. Martinson outlined more of his feelings in his letter:

> At home we have worked diligently to encourage Shane's interest in Science, as well as working on his organizational skills. Yet, for some reason, he seems reluctant, even unmotivated to embrace this particular course of study. I have enclosed a copy of a project Shane has completed for his Physical Education class. He took great care in researching and gathering information for this report. As you can see by the detail and care he has applied to this report, Shane obviously felt motivated and supported. Shane spent an entire evening researching the internet seeking just the right images and data to support his point.
>
> Given your years of teaching experience, if you have any ideas or suggestions on how to motivate Shane in your class, I would be happy to discuss them in person with you and Shane. You can reach me at xxx.xxx-xxxx to schedule a date and time to discuss and develop a support plan for Shane.
>
> Regards,
> Gavin Martinson
> Cc: Maria Garcia, 6th Grade Guidance Counselor

Mr. Martinson informed me that this teacher failed to respond to this letter and neglected further correspondence. The result of this unsuccessful communication led to Shane's lack of desire in science. This letter is an important reminder of how a lack of communication with parents can negatively affect a student's academic growth. In this case, it diminished Shane's interest in science because this teacher failed to communicate early on with Shane's parents, thereby prohibiting them from intervening in a timely manner.

Teachers Gave Excessive Suspensions and Detentions

Four participants reported that teachers gave excessive suspensions and detentions. Jeremiah fervently discussed his thoughts about his teachers and counselors who he felt unnecessarily suspended him constantly:

> A: Jeremiah, what do you think about all your experience in school? You can talk about your past experiences and your present experiences?

J: Well, in school like some teachers hate me, some teachers don't hate me. Some teachers want me to past, some teachers don't. But uh like, this counselor, for example this counselor named Ms. Healy she always suspended me for no reason. For example like, when I was at school this girl uh threw this ball at this uh boy and she blamed it on me and the boy told her that it was the girl but she still suspended on me and put a police, police report on me.

A: And what about the other teachers? How do you know that they don't want you to do good?

J: Because when I'm doing something, they don't tell me to stop it or she'll just yell at me and then try to write me up on a referral.

Jeremiah's account was typical in that he mentioned Ms. Healy as the cause of his unnecessary suspension. This was consistent with his mother's explanation of Ms. Healy stated earlier. In particular, he pointed out that she suspended him for no reason. This was key in that it reinforced Ms. Healy's unnecessary harassment of Jeremiah. I asked Jeremiah about other teachers who gave excessive suspensions and detentions:

A: When you say she, can you talk about this person who writes you up?

J: Her name is Ms. Howard and she's a teacher, she's a history teacher and she don't like me at all (raises voice).

A: And can you talk about this experience, can you talk about why she doesn't like you.

J: Well she show do uh, uh write a whole lot of referrals all over me, over stuff uh that I didn't do. But, then other kids she write, other kids referrals and things to. But other than that, I get more referrals than everybody in that class from her.

A: And why do you think she writes so many referrals about you. I mean are there specific reasons?

J: Yeah like, if we talkin' out loud or somebody over there playing a music on they phone they uh, then she'll blame it on me, or the kids will lie on me and say I did it, even though they know Imma get in trouble and still they, I still get in trouble for something that I didn't do.

A: And how does that make you feel when she writes a referral on you?

J: It makes me feel like kinda mad, sad, mad cause I didn't do it, she never believe me and that's the reason why (Interview with Jeremiah, Friday, June 6, 2008).

I found Jeremiah's comments about the other students in his class peculiar. It seemed as if they realized Ms. Howard's dislike of Jeremiah, using her dislike as a means to get Jeremiah into unnecessary trouble and then kicking him out of class.

Teachers Had Low Expectations for Students

Two participants stated that teachers had low expectations for students. Jerele talked about his experience with teachers who had low expectations:

A: You said that teachers kind of passed you through without really, you know uh concerned about your grades or concerned about you graduating. Can you talk about those experiences?

J: Well, I felt like the way they had passed me through school without learning it, was kind of failing. And one of the reasons why they did cause they didn't want to be bothered and they just wanted me to go on and didn't care if I got out or nothing. But at the end, they were all wrong (He smiles).

A: (I Laugh) I like that, and what was it, why do you think they wanted you to fail. Can you give some examples?
J: I think it was in middle school when it started because when I used to bring some, when I started out on an assignment, she'd say awe, just do a little bit, don't do all of it. So that's all I would do and then come back and she would just pass me on. He or she and (inaudible) wow.

Jerele described how teachers allowed him to pass without inspection - doing the minimum on homework assignments. I asked Jerele to elaborate on this teacher who had low expectations for him:

A: Can you talk a little more about this person. This experience, some of the things she used to do that would make you feel like uh, she was just passing you through.

J: Well, she didn't really care if I got it right or not, she just let me, let me slide through and I was like okay. And she didn't really care if I really graduated or not. That's how I know she didn't care (pauses). And that didn't feel so good (Interview with Jerele, Monday, June 2, 2008).

In this example above, Jerele described a specific incident that raised his critical consciousness about teachers who have low expectations. I was amazed by Jerele's realization about this concept in his life, because he observed the inadequacies of public school at such an early age in his academic career. In the same way, Jerele's mother corroborated his reflections in a conversation about low expectations:

> ...She expressed "in his elementary school, you know they tried to pass him on...you know...and I told them I did not appreciate the way they was treating Jerele Aaron...it seemed like they was feeling sorry for him because of his illness you know...but they was also doing the other Black kids like that...the ones who you know who struggled with certain subjects and everything like that...you know how they (referring to White teachers) do..." (Researcher's Journal, January 10, 2006).

Ms. Carter pointed to the fact that teachers felt sorry for Jerele because of his illness. As a result, they allowed Jerele to pass without scrutiny. Significantly, race was included in this explanation of teachers with low expectations, once again emphasizing the systemic racism that is prevalent in JUSD.

In summary, the data for Research Question #1 revealed more unsatisfactory than satisfactory responses for teacher-student relationships and academic experiences of African American males in public school. Most essential, the students' perceptions of systemic racism in the JUSD were included in the unsatisfactory responses. It is also important to note that individual teachers, not school policies or other explanations, were mentioned as the cause of unsatisfactory and satisfactory teacher-student relationships and academic experiences.

Research Question #2:

What Are the Tutor-Tutee Relationships and Academic Experiences of African American Males in an In-home, One-On-One Tutorial Situation?

Satisfactory Perceptions of Tutor-Tutee Relationships

Students Enjoyed Tutor

Two participants confirmed that students enjoyed their tutor. Dario's mother expressed her opinion about his tutor:

...She mentioned, "You just don't know Aaron...that boy really love you...it's like he can talk to you more than me...he need that part you know...his dad ain't around so he look to you for that guidance...you have done so much for him...he be getting ready for you way before you come now... (I started smiling). He be telling his brothers about ya tutoring." (Researcher's Journal, January 15, 2008).

Ms. Gatewood's comments brought forth the point that Dario looked up to me as a father figure. Her interpretation was humbling because I had no idea I inspired Dario to that extent.

Similarly, Shareek articulated his feelings about tutoring:

A: And how do you feel about your tutor?

S: (pauses for a moment) you care, you ain't, you really patient, that's what I like about you, you cain't be a tutor if you don't have no patience, and I can see you have patience a lot. Plus (inaudible) been slacking but you still have patience for me. And you never got mad, but you said like oh, you need to get it together, because you been slacking off (inaudible) and I like that cause you gotta have patience right to be a good tutor. And thats good to have and it's like you funny, you just like, (inaudible) you just got everything to be like a good teacher, you can be a teacher if you wanted to, I would love to come to your class you know, but yeah its like, you got patience its like a (inaudible) you just fun to just kick it with. And that's what I like about you (Interview with Shareek, Wednesday, June 4, 2008).

Shareek's position pointed to the fact that he enjoyed his tutor because of the patience he felt I gave him in tutoring. Shareek continued his explanation with more specific comments:

A: Can you talk about all your years or experience in tutoring. How do you feel about it?

S: I feel good. It's like (pauses) I learn new things like each time, like um math; I didn't know that much about division and then can I say its you (whispers)?

A: Sure, uh huh

S: You just taught me like more, you know, cuz I was like (inaudible) wow its really like that? And you explain stuff so good, that's what I like about it. So you know. I love that. If you can't, if you don't, some people be, some teachers be quick to say stuff. They be trying to be mixing it up.

A: Uh huh

S: You don't understand it. They be doing it on purpose some time. (Inaudible) try to not, unless you get it. But you do it like just perfect. So I can understand it like regularly. (Inaudible) Why people got to say like other stuff to mix you up? (Inaudible) what are you talking about? But you explain just normal. Like, that's what I like about it (Interview with Shareek, Wednesday, June 4, 2008).

Shareek enjoyed tutoring because of my ability to clarify, which helped him to better comprehend my lesson plans. Shareek's mother talked about my presence in his life:

...She told me "...Mr. Horn, thank you for all the work you do for Shareek...I have never seen him open up to someone so fast...He has been talking more and expressing himself more...I never seen him do this so fast...It's like you just have a certain affect on him...I can't explain it (she laughs aloud)...he really like you Mr. Horn...Thank you so much...You have been a blessing to Shareek...God Bless you Mr. Horn..." I felt honored that he liked me so much. She also mentioned that I was a good role model for Shareek and other Black kids. She stated, "For him to talk to you about personal stuff, it's really good. Shareek look at you as a role model...you just don't know Mr. Horn. You like they father, they teacher, they brother..." (Researcher's Journal, December 5, 2007).

Similar to Ms. Gatewood, Shareek's mother's insight left me bewildered because I was unaware that Shareek considered me a father figure. Jerele spoke about his fondness for being around me:

A: You said that your tutor is very patient. Can you describe something that makes you believe he's patient?

J: Aaron is patient with me in math because he knows, he knows that I need to understand it and he just sit down and works with it, helps me with it and he keeps going over and over with it until I get it right. And I feel like very thankful for that! (Interview with Jerele, Monday, June 2, 2008).

Comparable to Shareek, Jerele was appreciative of me because of the patience he felt I provided him in tutoring. Uncle Jake discussed his outlook about my presence in Taylor's life:

Taylor had another excellent month...I talked to his Uncle and he told me that his report card showed that Taylor improved drastically in reading. He thanked me for helping Taylor stay focused in school. He expressed, "I don't understand it...he love to be here with you...but not school. He don't wanna have anything to do with them teachers, especially Mr. Ancelman. He loves tutoring Aaron (raises voice loudly)...He seem like he learn more in tutoring than in school..."

Uncle Jake's discussion about Taylor's improved reading on his report card underscored the importance of how in-home, one-on-one tutoring could improve basic skills. Taylor's reading improved from the individual assistance I provided him as a tutor. Uncle Jake continued with more explanation for Taylor's liking of me:

> ...When I asked Uncle Jake to explain his reason for Taylor's interest in tutoring, he informed me, "I don't know...it's probably the way you talk to Taylor...cause it seem like he break ice wit chu more than me (breaking ice means talking about personal subjects)...I think it's good that he can have somebody to talk to other than me and his brothers." It was motivating to hear that Taylor trusts me so much. I really enjoy our personal conversations... (Researcher's Journal, November 13, 2007).

Although Taylor and I often talked about personal issues, I never understood the magnitude of our conversations. These comments from Uncle Jake helped me understand the importance of dialogue in Taylor's life. His enjoyment of discussing personal issues increased his desire to be around me more. Coincidently, Taylor requested I spend more time with him as a suggestion for improving my tutoring.

Tutor Encouraged Students

Five participants said that the tutor encouraged students. Dario verbalized his point of view about being encouraged:

> A: How do you feel your tutor wants you to do in school? Can you give an example?

> D: Um, because he wanted me to do good and he tells me and he just like, its like a good, it's just feel good to learn something new each day, and like when he tells me I do good, just, it feel, he or she tells me I do good, its just, it just make me, it just makes me feel better even more (Interview with Dario, Tuesday, June 3, 2008).

Dario's standpoint of tutoring emphasized that my encouragement influenced his attitude in a positive way.

Jerele's caregiver, Ms. Carter, talked about the way I encouraged Jerele:

> ...She stated, "That boy loves you man...you hear me...that boy loves you...he be smiling and grinning when you around...I love the way you take care of him Aaron... you know...you really inspire him to make him do better in school...he always asking me what would you think about this assignment or things like that....you can tell he look up to you...you know..." (Researcher's Journal, December 4, 2007).

Analogous to Dario, Ms. Carter illustrated how my encouragement increased Jerele's motivation for school and enjoyment for tutoring. Jeremiah communicated his feelings about the way I encouraged him:

> A: How do you feel during tutoring session?
>
> J: I feel like its helping me a lot and I feel like we cool, we could uh (inaudible) communicate with each other and things like that and then (pauses) and when we be like reading and stuff, he, when I, say I wanna quit, he push me to go on and on and more an more and make, he helps me a lot even if I'm doing bad in school. He even helps me a lot. He even come and get me and go, take me to the bookstore so I can study on some more history and things like that and pick out books to read.

Here again, my encouragement motivated Jeremiah to read more. Jeremiah further discussed his thoughts about being encouraged:

> A: How do you feel about your tutor?
>
> J: I feel good. He's a cool guy, intelligent and things. He help me out, very, push me to the limit to I cain't go no more and I thank him for that.
>
> A: Can you talk about pushing you to the limit. What is about your tutor that, that makes you feel he pushes you to the limit? What does that mean?
>
> J: He, he gives me more challenges even though I don't wanna do 'em and if I say I quit, he don't even and he tell me to, he, he, he tell me to keep goin and goin and goin, but then, sometimes I don't wanna go and quit, but sometimes I push, and he push me to the limit till I just have to do it (Interview with Jeremiah, Friday, June 6, 2008).

In this example, my encouragement motivated Jeremiah to persevere. Jeremiah's mother validated her son's belief about the way I encouraged him:

> ...She exclaimed, "You da best tutor ever (I start laughing)...he ain't never have no tutor like you Mr. Horn...you da best...He be trying harder cause of you...it's like he wanna learn more...you know...the curriculum

you give him...he be doing it on his own...he get so excited when you be coming...he just love working with you...keep doing what cha doing...you have been a big influence on my son...I thank God for you..." (Researcher's Journal, June 6, 2008).

Like Ms. Carter, Jeremiah's mother described how my encouragement motivated Jeremiah to improve his academics, particularly in the way he completed his tutoring curriculum. Shareek presented his view about encouragement:

A: How do you feel that your tutor wants you to do in school?

S: Well, I think you want me to do good. You always on me all the time, you know, like a dad. So yeah, I think you want me to do good in school. You want me to be focused, you want me to be organized, you want me to be all this, you know, just real prepared, you know, and all this stuff, for college, and for right now too (Interview with Shareek, Wednesday, June 4, 2008).

Parallel to Dario, Shareek categorized my encouragement as paternalistic. In this way, my encouragement inspired him on a more personal level.

Satisfactory Perceptions of In-Home Tutoring Academic Experiences

Improved Reading Skills

Three participants conveyed that students improved their reading skills in in-home tutoring. Shareek expressed his view on how tutoring improved his reading:

A: You mentioned that tutoring helped you in school. Can you give an example of what ways it's helped you?

S: Well like, I think reading is like a big part, cuz like, I can (inaudible) so many words. Like, its like, tutoring and the school helped me. Its like, (inaudible) that made it even more better, it's like, but tutoring is like, (inaudible) its a big part of it, and school is like, its like fifty-fifty (tutoring versus school) it was like, I don't know cus I was reading one thing one day and I came across a word, a big word, and then like I just pronounced it out whatever and I just got it, bam, like that. I was like, I was so amazed.

Shareek's perception represented how in-home tutoring improved his reading in school, specifically with word recognition. His clarification of how tutoring and school enhanced his reading symbolized the importance of how the coexistence of in-home tutoring and public schools enhanced academics for Shareek. Shareek talked more about his refined reading skills:

> S: I was like wow I really got that word, (inaudible) it was like some other kinda word (inaudible) it was like some big rich word, like nobody would ever even use (inaudible) just said it, (inaudible) and I got it, I was so amazed. And like, (sighs) when I went to that, when I came to that school I'm going to now, it's like my reading got so good and like everything, tutoring made me so, read so good, it's like everything, its like wow, Like Imma be (laughs) learning from school and tutoring and its like, and that's, that's good (Interview with Shareek, Wednesday, June 4, 2008).

Shareek was overwhelmingly excited about remembering a complex word during class. He expressed that he felt embarrassed to speak in class because he lacked reading comprehension skills. Since Shareek was able to practice his reading and vocabulary skills in tutoring, his confidence and self-esteem emanated in class. Shareek's mother corroborated Shareek's claim:

> ...She explained, "he reading more Mr. Horn...Shareek be asking to borrow my books...he also wrote me a poem about his father and all the stuff he did... Mr. Horn I started crying...He got it (the poem he wrote) in his tutoring binder in those plastic sheets that you gave him..." (Researcher's Journal, December 5, 2007).

In this case, Shareek's improved reading increased his ability to write through poetry. Ms. Carter spoke about Jerele's reading development:

> ...She said, "You gotta stay on dat boy Aaron...I like your style. I notice when we at the bookstore, he'll pick out a book about people and everything...he like them autobiographies...he'll read when you here...oh yeah (looks at me with a serious face)...he listens to you...I see him reading before you get here...I notice he like reading different books and everything with you....remember when ya'll read about Martin Luther King and what was her name again (I responded "Harriet Tubman")...yeah, that lady...he really enjoyed those type of books. It makes a difference when you read with him...I can tell..." (Researcher's Journal, February 20, 2007).

Ms. Carter's narrative demonstrated how my consistent reading with Jerele improved his aptitude and increased his interest in reading. Jerele became more interested in reading because of our consistent practices which included reading autobiographies of African Americans.

Learned about the African Diaspora

Six participants said they learned about Black history in tutoring. Jeremiah informed me of his knowledge:

> A: You said that you learned about people in tutoring. Can you talk about some of those people you learned about?

> J: Like I learned about Harriet Tubman, how she free, freed the slaves following the North Star and how when she was young that she got uh real serious uh injury by one of the slave owners and got her uh she can fall into deep sleeps and have blackouts and (whispers) things like that (Interview with Jeremiah, Friday, June 6, 2008).

Jeremiah's explicit details about Harriet Tubman exemplified his excitement for the Black history lessons in tutoring. Taylor described his newfound knowledge of Black history:

> A: Can you give an example of how you learn different things in tutoring?

> T: Yeah, well he teach me how to do math and spelling and he teach me how to write the definitions down and reads, old stories about people that, who helped are um, who helped the united states and the civils rights.

> A: Can you remember some assignments about those people? You said you learned about civil rights. Do you remember who we talked about?

> T: Um, Shaka Zulu and um Kelsey Morton (hesitates – the actual name is Kelly Miller).

> A: And what did those people do?

> T: Well, he, he Shaka Zulu he was a brave warrior and he, he kilt the people that didn't let his mom stay cause they, cause they didn't have no um, he didn't have no father and she didn't have no husband so they didn't let her stay, so she went into um exile (hesitates) and John, Kelsey Morton, he, he, he trying to keep the Black people back from going to a different state, but they wanted to leave but (exhales) and that's it (Interview with Taylor, Tuesday, June 3, 2008).

Although the accuracy of his knowledge was partial, Taylor remembered the major themes of each lesson. Taylor's description validated his fondness for Black history.

Students Acquired Life Skills

Four participants communicated that students acquired life skills in in-home tutoring.

Improved trust of Black males. Ms. Gatewood talked about Dario's improved trust for Black males which she believed he obtained in in-home tutoring:

> ...She explained, "you gotta understand something...and I mean this...Dario has never really trusted people until he met you, especially Black men...now he be acting better with men...you feel me...Black men...he used to hate men but now you gave him stability because...you know...your consistency, so now he trust men.... he used to never believe in men but until he met you he changed...you feel me...I mean...he more confident in himself and he believes in Black men now..."

Ms. Gatewood's position about Dario trusting Black men was inspiring. Because Dario lacked male guidance, he had never been able to trust men, Black men in particular. Her comments about our relationship drew attention to the significance of how my mentorship with Dario influenced his point of view. Dario was able to trust Black men because of his successful relationship with an older Black male. Dario's mother continued to explain the influence of my presence:

> ...She expressed, "He is so excited about you Aaron...he cain't wait to see you so to me...you make him better...It took him a long time to trust people after his grandfather died and his father left him but now he be opening up more with you..." I was relieved to hear Ms. Gatewood's opinion because Dario has been expressing himself more in tutoring and I was wondering if he was becoming more trusting of me... (Researcher's Journal, March 25, 2008).

Ms. Gatewood's belief was influential because trust is central in developing academic relationships, especially a tutor-tutee relationship. Dario was able to trust me because of my consistency – my ability to show up.

Similarly, Shareek expressed his trust of me as a Black male:

A: You mentioned that you feel your tutor cares; can you give an example of how he showed that he cared, like a specific example?

S: ...I felt so comfortable with you, it was like, you know, I felt you was there for me, so that felt like you cared for me, so yeah, I can talk to you

about whatever's on my mind, you know, and there's that connection...
(Interview with Shareek, Wednesday, June 4, 2008).

Shareek's reflection shed light on the importance of building trust. In this example, Shareek felt comfortable to share personal experiences because of the care demonstrated by his tutor.

Improved focus. Dario talked about the impact of in-home tutoring on his school experience:

> A: Umkay and you talked about being calm and quiet in tutoring last time. Can you talk more about that?
>
> D: Cause it keeps me on task in school. I just think I'm tutoring, but except with all the other kids.
>
> A: So, do you mean that tutoring helps you do better in school?
>
> D: Yes, that's what I mean? (Interview with Dario, Tuesday, June 3, 2008).

Dario's comments give a clear description of how in-home tutoring increased his focus in school.

Improved motivation for school. Ms. Morris spoke about Jamie's improved desire to go to school:

> ... "that boy, always be talking about you Aaron...every time we bring up school, he mention yo name...it seems like you helped him get his confidence back in school...you hear me...(I started smiling)...you know...it seems like he wanna be there now.... Sheila (Jamie's mom) and I really thank you for all the work you do for that boy..."(Researcher's Journal, May 23, 2007).

Ms. Morris's point of view clarified how the mere presence of someone can motivate students. In this circumstance, Jamie's enjoyment of my company, associating academics with my name, encouraged him to attend school. Shane's father expressed his feelings about Shane's recent motivation:

> ..." Yeah, I think he's beginning to open up to you more...he has been through a lot in his life...I'm so glad he is trusting you more...we (Gavin's partner) were worried because he has so many issues around abandonment..."

Although Shane had the unique experience of having two males in his life, Mr. Martinson believed that Shane was still conflicted from abandonment issues. In this way, establishing a relationship with Shane was essential for successful tutoring. Mr. Martinson added:

> "...he needed a Black male in his life...Shane is a tough one...I can see how your tutoring is working...he's starting to become more interested in his multiplication again...that's what he needs you know...somebody to get him motivated about math..." (Researcher's Journal, February 13, 2008).

Mr. Martinson's depiction called attention to the value of trust in a tutor-tutee relationship. Mr. Martinson attributed Shane's interest in math to his trust for me.

Felt empowered. Shareek articulated that he felt empowered by in-home tutoring:

> A: How do you feel during tutoring?

> S: I mean sometimes, I have my days, you know, I'm just tired. But, I feel good. Its Like, I feel (pauses) like, I feel so, I don't know, its just, I feel ready to learn. Like I'm just, empowered. Like, Like Cuz I'm, cuz you teach so good, it's like, I already know Imma learn something new each day, every week.

> A: Why would you say you feel that way? Why do you feel empowered or ready to learn? Why do you feel that way?

> S: Because it's like, I don't know, I'm so comfortable with you? It's like, you know, you know, you a good teacher. And so its like, (inaudible) that's why I feel like that?

> A: And how do you feel after tutoring has ended um everyday, how do you feel?

> S: I feel good cuz its like, you do all this work and you get something out of it cuz its like you learning something. And yeah, and that's just a good thing to have. Like, uh to actually learn something. And you see out there is what you learned is like alright that's not easy no more, I mean that's not hard no more. Its actually, I get it now, every time somebody give me a paper about it, I (inaudible) just like that. You aint sure about it no more, you just know it, you can just do it, like just like that. That's a good feeling to have (Interview with Shareek, Wednesday, June 4, 2008).

Shareek felt empowered because his knowledge base was enhanced through in-home tutoring. In particular, he enjoyed the comfortable environment that in-home tutoring provided him. Consequently, he felt more capable of completing school assignments with confidence.

Increased organizational skills. Jerele spoke about his improved organizational skills:

> A: And you also mentioned that you learned a lot about organization in tutoring. Can you talk about that?
>
> J: Organizing helped me a lot cause now I don't have to, I don't have, I can move, I move forward. I don't have stuff all over, all over the kitchen table. Instead, I can keep this pile right here and that pile right here. And I don't, and I don't have to go through piles looking for something. Cause when I just have an assignment and I need to get the previous one, I just go right there and take it out. (Interview with Jerele, Monday, June 2, 2008).

Prior to my tutoring, Jerele failed his classes because he did not turn in homework assignments. After being taught how to organize in in-home tutoring, Jerele's newly acquired life skill helped systematize his homework.

Unsatisfactory Perceptions of Relationships and Academic Experiences

No participants communicated unsatisfactory perceptions of tutor-tutee relationships and academic experiences of African American males in in-home, one-on-one tutoring. On the contrary, student participants notably had suggestions to improve in-home, one-on-one tutoring (See Research Question #4, Page 97, for responses).

The data for Research Question #2 revealed only satisfactory responses for tutor-tutee relationships and academic experiences of African American males in in-home, one-on-one tutoring. Essential to all of these satisfactory responses was the explicit description of the tutor as patient and encouraging. What I found striking was how the student participants and parents isolated life skills as the most influential. In all the data, Shareek gave the most profound response. His description about how his reading skills improved through the collaboration of in-home tutoring and public school clarified the purpose of my study.

Research Question #3:

How Do Students Compare Their Relationships and

Academic Experiences in Public School with In-Home, One-On-One Tutoring?

Satisfactory Comparisons of Teacher-Student and Tutor-Tutee Relationships

Four participants stated that students enjoyed their teachers and tutor. Dario declared his reasons:

> A: How do you compare your relationships with your teacher to your relationships with your tutor? Can you talk about those relationships?

> D: I think they're good and fun and that's mostly all I have to say about the teachers and tutoring. They're really fun and cool.

> A: Can you give an example about fun and cool? What is your definition of fun and cool?

> D: Um, I think that their fun and cool and because I learn a lot and, and just get a lot of the stuff from learning a lot and being good. That's all I have to say (Interview with Dario, Tuesday, June 3, 2008).

Dario's teachers and tutor made his academic experience fun. Because of teachers' and tutor's pleasurable conduct, Dario learned more in class. Dario's mother gave a more specific reason for his enjoyment of tutoring:

> ...She expressed, "He always talk about how he want to be with you...He like that stability you provide...I think he needs that to be honest with you...I mean he just like being able to go with you and get away from the house (referring to his Grandmother's house)..he need that...you feel me..." (Researcher's Journal, November 13, 2007).

Dario's mother pointed out that Dario enjoyed the one-on-one element of tutoring. The mere companionship with his tutor made tutoring enjoyable. Similar to Dario, Jeremiah verified why he likes his teachers and tutor:

> A: How do you compare your relationships with your teacher to your relationships with your tutor?

> J: Whelp, like some of my teachers is cool, and my tutor he cool. Like some, he, he want to push me, like my other teachers want to push me to the limit. Like they want a, want me to graduate and have good jobs...

> A: Okay and when you say cool, can you maybe elaborate on that, like what do you mean by cool?

J: Like their intelligent and they teach you more and more even though you don't want to listen but they keep teaching you until they cain't teach you no more (Interview with Jeremiah, Friday, June 6, 2008).

Both Jeremiah's teachers and tutor motivated him to exceed in academics. He enjoyed his teachers and tutor so much that he wanted to find a good job. Jamie gave a variety of reasons why he enjoyed his teachers and tutor:

A: How do you compare your relationships with your teacher to your relationships with your tutor?

J: Well, tutor is a funner person and the teacher, its juts the same thing but the tutor is a little better because its funner and you can joke around with the tutor sometimes and with teachers you really cant because their trying to teach you and they got a schedule to do.

A: Umkay, so you feel that your tutor, you, you can joke around with this person more than your teacher?

J: Yes

A: Can you give an example or an experience where you feel good with your tutor?

J: Well one experience when I talked about this girl Ashley and for valentines and he was nice enough to give me a rose but he didn't have to do that cause that was his.

A: I noticed that you said, in comparing relationships you said that it's funner with your tutor. Can you maybe even elaborate on more of those relationships?

J: Cause he feels like my best friend, like a big buddy.

A: And could you maybe elaborate on that more. Like, what do you mean by that?

J: Like when, when we just got done doing something, give me a high five or a good job, you did this. But with some people they be like, oh okay let's just go to the next thing (lowers voice).

A: Okay, and

J: He make, he make me feel a little better.

Although Jamie wavered in his opinion, he enjoyed both his tutor and teacher because he felt they were fun to be around. On the other hand, he felt more at ease with his tutor. Jamie's recollection of my ability to connect with his feelings about Valentine's Day seemed most pertinent because I tried to connect with all of my tutees on a personal level, especially when I felt they cared about something important in their life. Jamie talked more about his fondness for his teachers and tutor:

> A: Okay, And what about your relationships with your teachers? Can you talk about those a little more?

> J: Well, the one at Martin Luther King, Mr. Roland, he's good, he's not like Aaron but he's good. He, he jokes around a little but not that much. Cause he really want to get, get all that um stuff he could learn, I mean stuff he could teach to the kids. Cause he is strict (Interview with Jamie, Thursday, June 5, 2008).

Jamie enjoyed his teacher because of his firmness. Although he learned in both environments, he felt his teacher was less fun than his tutor. Jerele gave an account of his affection for his teachers and tutor:

> A: And how do you compare your relationships with your teacher to your relationships with your tutor?

> J: My relationships to Ms. Manbahs to, and Aaron are, are (pauses) are excellent. They both help me, they both tell me what I need to do and what I'm working, and what I need to work on. You know their kinda like my, their kinda like, their good helpers (swallows).

> A: And can you explain a little bit more of that. You said they

> J: Well, for example Ms. Manbahs says I can come after school and work on the computers and Aaron just comes right after, right after, right after I get off school and just helps me with my tutoring, tutor me. So it's kind of like an after school tutoring but different places (Interview with Jerele, Monday, June 2, 2008).

Jerele's beliefs about his teachers and tutor were similar in that he felt they both helped him equally.

Satisfactory Comparisons of Public School and In-Home Tutoring Experiences

Three participants discussed their enjoyment of public school and tutoring. Jeremiah articulated his view:

> A: Do you prefer public school or in-home tutoring and why do you prefer which one?

> J: Whelp, I prefer uh public school because it's more people around you and a bigger environment and, I, I like I want in-home uh tutoring too because like the tutor more like more things than the school people do and then like when you go to school you already know the answers to things and (inaudible) it really help you so I'll have both if I have to really have to chose I really chose tutoring or I don't know, because it don't, but I really want both because it helps me out more and more each day.

Even though Jeremiah vacillated in his descriptions about public school and in-home tutoring, he enjoyed both for different reasons. He liked public school for the larger environment, more access to peers, and in-home tutoring for the extracurricular activities. In this illustration, public school and in-home tutoring jointly enhanced the academic experience of Jeremiah. He continued to compare both experiences:

> A: Umkay, so it sounds like you want both environments?

> J: Yes sir!

> A: And how will both environments help you academically and in your personal life?

> J: It will help me go through college, get degrees, high school get all that, and cuz you already know everything, and you ain't got to go worry about asking the teacher. You do yo work and then you'll be an A plus student (Interview with Jeremiah, Friday, June 6, 2008).

While Jeremiah's description of collaboration by public school and in-home tutoring sounded unusual, his point further emphasized their combined impact on his academic experience. The collaborative effort increased his interest in college and performance in school. Shareek told a similar comparison of in-home tutoring and public school:

> A: Do you prefer your school or do you prefer in-home tutoring? And why

do you prefer you know which one that you choose?

S: Dam, that's a hard uh, that's a hard question cuz in both, in tutoring and my new school is like I'm both learning something. Dam, um, (smacks teeth) dam I don't know which one I would pick but you know. If you was working at my school, I would pick my uh school though. But I can't choose both (laughs). I can't choose one of them without choosing the other one. But if it was a decision to my old school and my school, my new school, I would pick my new school. And if it was a decision to my old school and you, I would pick you though. Cuz my old school is not even in the category though. Fa real (Interview with Shareek, Wednesday, June 4, 2008).

Shareek's estimation of both environments clarified the influence that academic environments had on his educational experience. He clearly enjoyed his new public school because of the stimulating environment. On the other hand, he stated he would choose in-home tutoring over his old school. What was interesting was that he struggled to select one academic environment over the other.

Unsatisfactory Comparisons of Teacher-Student and Tutor-Tutee Relationships

One participant, Taylor, stated his preference for the tutor. He expressively pronounced his preference:

A: And how do you compare your relationships with your teachers to your relationship with tutor?

T: I be telling 'em, telling them (his elementary school teachers) that he (his tutor) teach me more than ya. And ya don't really, ya just sit up there and help the fifth graders and don't (inaudible) help me and they just, they say who teach you more and I say my tutor and I always tell 'em I got tutor on Wednesday so I tell em I don't need ya help no more.

A: Wow, so you actually tell your teachers that your tutor is better than them?

T: Yes

A: And why do you feel that way?

T: Because they don't help me. They just help the fifth graders.

A: Okay so you mean they help the fifth, while you're in class with fifth graders, they help the fifth graders more than they do the fourth graders or more than they do you?

T: More than they do me.

Taylor clarified his preference for his tutor. He believed that his teachers did not help him and felt his tutor taught him better. His boldness to tell his teachers about their inadequacies was extraordinary. Although his comments were inappropriate, I commended him for expressing himself. Taylor talked about one specific teacher he disliked:

> …Taylor had a terrific month…As usual, Taylor informed me that he dislikes Mr. Ancelman. He does not like the way Mr. Ancelman treats him. He told me, "he don't know how to handle his class (I look at him with amazement and laugh)….he don't…he be yelling at the kids and they don't be listening to him….

Taylor's bravery to vividly describe his dislike for his teachers was admirable. His dislike for Mr. Ancelman was consistent. Taylor was able to make what I believe was an astute observation about Mr. Ancelman – his inability to control his classroom. Taylor's observation was impressive because it showed his ability to be conscious about the specific teaching qualities of teachers. His uncle validated Taylor's claim:

> …Immediately after our meeting, I spoke with Uncle Jake about Taylor's candidness. Uncle Jake expressed, "Man…that's how it be Aaron…(he laughs)… I mean Taylor…he don't wanna listen to nobody but you…It seem like Mr. Ancelman just be yelling at them kids for no reason…you know… I mean I be going to visit Taylor and he be quiet when I'm there but man you should see them other Black kids…how they be running around his class Aaron… (Raises voice) I mean the whole class be screaming and talking to dat man (Mr. Ancelman) all kinds a ways…cursing him out and everything…I mean they did it in front of me …I don't understand it… (Researcher's Journal, February 20, 2007).

I found Uncle Jake's estimation of Taylor's preference for his tutor surprising because it reflected a level of respect that should also have been given to Mr. Ancelman. This example demonstrated that he appreciated his tutor more than Mr. Ancelman. This may be caused in part by our trusting relationship versus a distrusting relationship with Mr. Ancelman.

Unsatisfactory Comparisons of Public School and In-Home Tutoring Experiences

Three participants said they preferred in-home tutoring over public school. Shareek described his preference for in-home tutoring:

> A: And why would you choose me over your old school?

> S: Cuz, dam, I mean like, at my old school, I wasn't learning nothing (voice raises). Like not, nothing at all. Not no, just, just, just nothing like (laughs). Just, God, don't wanna even be there. And in tutoring, its like, I wanna be here. I mean, I might slack off a little but you know I still wanna be here. I still wanna learn something. And I do learn something everyday that, that you come. And then when I go there (his old school), I just wanna cut, you know, just wanna hang out, you know, just chill with my friends, and when the bell ring, I be like, I wanna be out. Don't wanna even stay there, forget it. I'm out. When the bus come, I'm just going up there. (Laughs) I don't even wanna be at my old school.

In his former school Shareek did not learn anything because he felt he was not stimulated by the environment. His preference for in-home tutoring stemmed from his enthusiasm and desire to learn something new. The new knowledge acquired in in-home tutoring motivated Shareek to learn more and be present at tutoring. Shareek clarified his thoughts:

> A: What was it about the in-home tutoring that you received from me, you know, the education, and versus, compared to your old school?

> S: Well, tutoring, it was just more hands on. More attention and you explain the work good. You know that's what I like. You know, I always like that. You know. It was just like. Dam, you know more hands on everything. You know. Old school, you know, they didn't do nothing, you know, with so many people acting up in the class. They couldn't even teach shit. Teachers (inaudible), teachers didn't know how to rule they class. You know, it was like, they didn't know how to teach. Dam, small little classrooms, I mean, it wasn't even that much people in the classroom and they still didn't know how to teach the class and how to control the class. I mean what you there for then (smack teeth). Dam, don't waist my time (Interview with Shareek, Wednesday, June 4, 2008).

Shareek's preference for in-home tutoring was motivated by his fondness for the tutor. More specifically, he enjoyed the tutor's ability to explain and assist him with assignments. Similar to Taylor, Shareek was frustrated that the teacher in his former school could not manage his peers, underscoring the need for more teacher training on classroom management. Jerele discussed his preference for in-home tutoring:

> A: Do you prefer in-home tutoring or do you prefer public school?

> J: I prefer in-home tutoring because, (pauses) because it's quiet. No noise, no kids, no kids shouting at each other and I can really work with it, and its calm (swallows twice) (Interview with Jerele, Monday, June 2, 2008).

Jerele's preference for in-home tutoring drew from his affection for a quiet atmosphere. Having worked with Jerele for ten years, I came to know his personality traits, especially his love of being alone and wanting personal attention. In in-home tutoring Jerele could get personal attention from one person without having to be interrupted by the noise of peers. In this case, Jerele chose the atmosphere of in-home tutoring for the tranquility. His mother validated his preference:

> ...She mentioned, "you know he likes tutoring more because of that you know...that one-on-one thang...that's how come I like your style of tutoring...you know...especially when ya be visiting them colleges...oh boy, that make Jerele excited baby...he be talking bout dat all night...you know...the way you teach him about organization, and read with him...I'm telling you..." (Researcher's Journal, March 24, 2008).

Ms. Carter's belief disclosed that Jerele enjoyed tutoring because of the individual attention he receives. Taylor described his preference for in-home tutoring:

> A: What do you think about in-home tutoring compared to school? Do prefer going to school or do you prefer in-home tutoring?

> T: Home tutoring.

> A: And why do you prefer in-home tutoring to school?

> T: Because its better and I learn more.

> A: And when you say better, can you explain that. What do you mean better?

T: Like I learn more and I do much harder things than I do at school (Interview with Taylor, Tuesday, June 3, 2008).

Taylor's preference for in-home tutoring was reminiscent of Shareek in that Taylor was also stimulated by the learning environment of in-home tutoring. He believed the work in in-home tutoring was more challenging than public school. For that reason, he was more excited about in-home tutoring. Having worked with Taylor for three years, I completely understood his appreciation for challenging homework. On many occasions, he expressed that I increase the difficulty of certain assignments, particularly math. This personal standard of achievement greatly impressed me, which is why I believed Taylor was a scholar. As a tutor, I learned from Taylor to never assume the academic level of tutees because their learning capacity would change at any moment.

In general, the data for Research Question #3 revealed that student participants and parents had more positive than negative comparisons of in-home tutoring and public school. Most fundamental within the data comparing teacher-student and tutor-tutee relationships were care and high expectations demonstrated by teachers and the tutor. These were the underpinnings of student participants' responses. Regardless of the humor incorporated in a lesson plan and the solicitation of students to study after school, student participants stated that teachers and their tutor wanted them to improve academically. Apart from the larger environment of public school and the tranquility of in-home tutoring, student participants expressed that they enjoyed both environments.

Research Question #4:

What Recommendations Would Students Make for

Improving In-Home, One-On-One Tutoring?

Recommendations for Improving Tutor-Tutee Relationships

Two participants said that they wanted the tutor to spend more time with students. Dario's mother discussed the following:

.... She stated, "You doing so good... I ain't got anything to complain about...(we both start to laugh)...if you give me something to complain about, then I'll complain...I mean...I would like to see you guys go to the movies more and hang out more...like I said...he needs that attention...I mean he like spending time with you...I notice when you tell him that you have to go and get your other students he get jealous...he need that one-on-one attention from you..." (Researcher's Journal, May 8, 2007).

Ms. Gatewood's comments underlined the importance of spending more time with Dario so he could feel special and admired. In the same way, Taylor expressed his thoughts:

A: In what ways can your tutor improve on his tutoring? What ways can I be a better tutor?

T: By helping me (smiles) and doing what he have to do for me and staying in my life to help me?

A: Umkay, and I've heard you talk about that before, about staying in your life. What does that mean?

T: By like helping me and being like an uncle to me, or a father and doing everything that he has to do for me to help me learn more (Interview with Taylor, Tuesday, June 3, 2008).

Taylor's description was comparable to Shareek who noted my paternalistic role in his life. Taylor felt that I needed to spend more time with him like a father in addition to being his tutor. In this way, he was declaring how I should be with him.

Recommendations for Improving Academic Experiences

More Challenging Work

One participant stated that he wanted more demanding homework. Taylor talked about his request:

> A: And what things would you change about tutoring to help, to make it even better.

> T: More harder.

> A: Umkay, and why do you feel that way?

> T: Because I get to learn more. (Interview with Taylor, Tuesday, June 3, 2008).

More Reading

As recorded in my journal, Taylor's uncle explained his feelings about wanting more reading:

> ...He expressed, "Ya'll cool...my only thing is because they ain't (Taylor's elementary school) teaching really nothing in that school, I would like to see ya'll read even more in tutoring. I mean I know you only got a certain amount of time...I understand that but what I'm saying is I would like that time to be used mainly for reading because he ain't gone learn it in his school...you understand what I'm saying..." (Researcher's Journal, May 6, 2008).

Uncle Jake's comment played up the need for more reading in Taylor's life, since he didn't feel that Taylor would receive ample reading in school.

Have a Classroom for Tutees

One participant said that he wanted tutees to have a classroom. Shareek shared his thoughts:

> A: And um, (clears throat) the second question is what things would you change about tutoring uh, to make it even better?

> S: Um, I probably (pauses) have the tutor like, have like they own classroom

> A: uh huh

S: where all the kids can just meet up at and he can just teach us, like, oh, they don't have to do it every like day but every like time, everyday but they can have like one time every, all the kids can just meet and he probably just teach em or just hang out with them, or whatever, that'll be cool

A: Oh, okay

S: Have his own little program and stuff like that

A: Uh hum

S: Yeah, that'll be cool though (Interview with Shareek, Wednesday, June 4, 2008).

Shareek's response highlighted the need for in-home tutoring to have an autonomous space in addition to the home environment.

Early Tutoring Schedule

One participant, Jerele, discussed that he wanted an earlier tutoring schedule:

A: And what things would you change about tutoring to make it even better?

J: I would have earlier scheduling, like (pauses and swallows) like right home, like right after I get from home from school to have him come, to have him come right away or something. (Interview with Jerele, Monday, June 2, 2008).

Jerele's response spoke to the need for incorporating more flexibility in the in-home tutoring schedule.

Study More Often

One participant, Dario, said he wanted to study more frequently with his tutor:

A: Okay, and what about, what things would you change about tutoring to make it better?

D: I would change about tutoring to make it better is that we could just study more often and um and just having a good time. (Interview with Dario, Tuesday, June 3, 2008).

Dario's reflection shed light on the importance of time in tutoring. Having more time would allow tutees to comprehend assignments and give them more personal attention. Jamie's mother expressed similar needs for her son:

> ...She informed me, "baby...we need you...don't give up on Jamie...He be hurtin' a lot okay from his brothers death (Jamie's older brother who died by gunshot)...I don't think he grieved Mr. Horn...I think you guys should go out and hang out more...I wish I could pay you more. I'm trying to see if I could get some more money so Jamie can see you more..." (Researcher's Journal, April 23, 2008.)

Jamie's mother comments showed the significance of individual attention. She felt that Jamie would have benefited from spending more personal time with me, especially since she believed Jamie had not overcome his brother's death.

The data from Research Question #4 showed that in-home tutoring needed reform for many reasons. Consistent in these recommendations were the need for additional resources, in particular more personal time with the tutor. Most significant was the request for a classroom in which tutoring could be held. Some tutees might have been uncomfortable with studying in the home environment; thereby emphasizing the importance for in-home, one-on-one tutoring to be more diversified in its location.

Summary

This chapter revealed that student participants and their parents had more negative than positive thoughts about public school. Particularly, three student participants revealed one incident of inadequate education involving an Asian teacher. In contrast, student participants and their parents had more positive than negative thoughts of in-home, one-on-one tutoring. Notably, five student participants shared that their tutor encouraged them. When comparing public school and in-home tutoring, student participants and their parents expressed more positive than negative assessments. Student participants and their parents suggested a variety of improvements for in-home, one-on-one tutoring. Two student participants stressed the need for more time with the tutor. By offering clear descriptions of ways to improve public school and in-home tutoring, this data lays the foundation for further implications to be discussed in Chapter VI.

CHAPTER VI

DISCUSSION, RECOMMENDATIONS, AND CONCLUSION

The findings in Chapter V showed that participants: (a) had more negative than positive opinions of public school; (b) had more positive than negative opinions of in-home, one-on-one tutoring; (c) communicated more positive comparisons with public school and in-home, one-on-one tutoring; and (d) articulated a variety of improvements for in-home, one-on-one tutoring.

As a result of these findings, this study provides creative ways to remedy the inadequate education of African American males, especially those in urban schools. In this chapter, I discuss the findings in relation to the research literature, offer recommendations for future research and practice, and present a final conclusion.

Discussion

The Positive Influence of Care

The positive influence of care was prevalent throughout the findings. Student participants and their parents stated that they enjoyed the care that teachers and tutors demonstrated to students. In the data on public school experiences, participants discussed that teachers encouraged students. Public school teachers need to encourage African American males consistently because this type of care can improve students' academic and teacher-student relationship experiences. This finding aligns with Dance (2002), whose research proves that African American males show more concern in school once they have a teacher who cares. Those few caring teachers that student participants experienced could be some of the reasons why my student participants remained in school.

Similarly, the positive impact of care can be seen in the data on comparing their experiences in public school and in-home, one-on-one tutoring. Student participants and parents believed both public school teachers and tutors demonstrated care and high expectations for students. Student participants and parents also stated that students were engaged in school and tutoring because of the teachers' and tutor's ability to care. The importance of care is salient in Fashola's (2005) work, which asserts that close teacher-student relationships must be demonstrated in the practice of teaching. Fashola also explains that the person who is charged with teaching African American males is just as important as the syllabus, school environment, and teacher training.

The most profound data about the positive influence of care came from participants and their parents who mentioned that the tutor was like a father figure to students, offering what I term "father-like care." Two participants and their parents stated that the father-like care demonstrated by the tutor positively influenced students' academic and relationship experience. Shareek discussed that the tutor's father-like care was illustrated by the tutor's ability to challenge him consistently to complete homework assignments. In other words, the father-like care was manifested through the tutor's inspiration. On a personal level, I understand the importance of the role that my student participants have assigned me because many African American males, including most of my tutees and myself, had no presence of a father in their lives. What makes this caring relationship so unique is that I come from the same neighborhoods as my students, helping me understand and relate to their academic and relationship experiences.

This type of caring relationship is similar to Dance's (2002) description of the type of teachers African American males gravitated to in her research. Dance describes these teachers as caring/empathetic teachers who genuinely care for students and understand the streets. This significance of care can be verified in the research by Bondy and Davis (2000), who found that students become more interested in their academics when a tutor expresses care for the students.

The Positive Influence of an Experienced Adult

The second most common theme that emerged from the data was the positive impact of an experienced adult, which translated into participants acquiring life skills, becoming more interested in reading, and increasing their reading scores. The teaching of life skills relates to Vygotsky's (1978) Zone of Proximal Development which states that the learning development of a child occurs within a relationship between a child and a more advanced peer or adult. It is within this interaction that a child achieves understanding. Through a trusting relationship, students achieved a level of mastery of life skills that can help to navigate the turbulent circumstances of their schools and communities.

Furthermore, participants and their parents stated that the tutor helped increase students' interest in reading and increased their test scores. These findings are comparable to Madden and Slavin's (2001) study, which showed that students' reading scores increased with the assistance of one-on-one tutoring. In addition, the authors explained that students were able to gain the necessary attention to build on their particular reading limitations because of the one-on-one tutoring. These findings are also related to Hock et al. (2001), whose study pointed out that middle school students increased their quiz and test scores because of one-on-one tutoring. What is more interesting in my findings was that student participants and parents stated tutor-tutee relationships as one important reason for students' increased motivation for reading and increased reading scores. In Vygotskyan (1978) theory, the experienced adult, the tutor, increased the reading skills of the tutees through their relationship.

The Negative Influence of a Lack of Care

From all the responses related to their negative perceptions of public schooling, the most common was lack of care towards students. This lack of care was manifested through racist treatment. Racism was the most common obstacle to adequate education students received in public school. For instance, Jamie's elementary school teacher described him as being "too big" for an elementary school age African American male. This type of racist description can create negative perceptions among other teachers who may then view Jamie as a threat to their classroom, leading to misplacement in special education. Jamie's experience verifies the findings of Kunjufu (2005), who reports that African American males are disproportionately placed in special education on the basis of teachers' misperceptions.

The most disturbing example of lack of care was Jamie's mistreatment by his elementary school teacher, who racially profiled him on a regular basis and even went to the extreme of isolating him in a closet. Jamie's mistreatment by this teacher could have allowed his other teachers to perceive him as so troubling that he must be feared and secluded from his peers, making this type of neglect standardized. Jamie's mistreatment can be rooted in the causes identified in the work by Ladson-Billings (1994). The author writes that when teachers demonstrate a lack of care, particularly racism, the perception of Black males among other teachers, administrators, and new teachers becomes misconstrued.

Another example of racism against students comes from the experience of Jeremiah with his middle school counselor. His counselor excessively categorized him as a troublemaker, placed him in detention, and suspended him. What is more disturbing is that Jeremiah's mother knew about this teacher's racist attitude for years because her other children attended the same school as Jeremiah. This generational racism demonstrated by Jeremiah's counselor can be explained by Kunjufu (2005) and Noguera (2005), who make clear that many African American males will experience racism at some point in mainstream education. This finding also calls attention to the systemic practice of racism in JUSD, which is consistent with Ladson-Billings and Tate (1995), who posit that school inadequacy is the cause of structural and institutional racism.

Recommendations for Future Research

Based on the responses from the student participants, I am recommending further research be conducted on father-like care, attachment theory, teacher perceptions, and identity development.

Father-like Care

In this study, father-like care emerged as the most prevalent form of care which appeared to have the most positive impact on students. Given this finding, more research needs to be conducted on father-like care and its effects on African American males. For example, when the tutor practiced this type of father-like care, students showed more interest in school and in-home, one-on-one tutoring. It appeared student participants enjoyed this type of care the most because of the absence of fathers in their lives. More importantly, student participants shared life experiences with the tutor that they had not shared with anyone else. Case in point, Taylor's uncle expressed that Taylor talks to me about his inadequate educational experiences more than anyone else. Because Taylor's father has been in jail since he was born, Taylor has not had a consistent male in his life other than his Uncle Jake. Although Taylor appreciates his Uncle Jake, Taylor has not been able to connect on a personal level with his uncle. His uncle often reminds me of the way Taylor admires and trusts me.

The caring relationship established between Taylor and me has allowed Taylor to trust me enough to share his experiences candidly without limits. In this way, the father-like care which I practice has allowed Taylor to trust and connect on a deeper level with an adult African American male. For this reason, father-like care needs to be investigated and further defined so that educators can find more ways to improve the inadequate education of young African American males. Future research on father-like care may be particularly useful to policymakers and practitioners in that incorporation of care can be implemented as policy after being clearly defined, thereby becoming meaningful to educational scholars.

Attachment Theory

After reviewing the data from student participants and my researcher journals, I delved further into the importance of interpersonal relationships. Regardless of the care demonstrated by the adults in the tutees' lives (e.g., tutor, mentor, teacher, and parent), tutees sometimes rejected attempts to establish a caring relationship. For example, I found that Shareek developed a type of separation anxiety concerning our tutoring relationship. I remember in December 2007, Shareek missed several of our tutoring appointments and failed to call to provide an explanation or apology. Later that month, I talked with his mother about Shareek's unusual behavior. Ms. Harris mentioned that Shareek was becoming anxious about tutoring, asking her if I was going to be in his life forever. Ms. Harris was overwhelmed because she was afraid Shareek was becoming emotionally unstable. She pleaded that I talked with Shareek in order to lessen his anxiety.

Shortly after my conversation with Ms. Harris, I took Shareek out for dinner and we talked extensively about my tutoring, especially the authenticity of my care. I remember being very honest and telling him that I am always accessible for all my students regardless if they remain on my caseload or not. He opened up about his father not being around and talked at length about his brother's death. After several months of inconsistent tutoring following our dinner, Shareek began trusting our relationship more. He showed up for tutoring on time and was prepared for each lesson. Although he has since dropped out of tutoring, I continue to see him every week as a mentor. We often go out for long walks to discuss personal issues. Similar to the trusting and caring tutor-tutee relationship we established, we seem to be developing the same type of mentor-mentee relationship.

Bowlby (1969) discusses that a child develops an attachment with his caregiver until they reach adolescence. At adolescence, they began to detach and form other healthy or secure attachments with other adults, organizations, and peers. The problem arises when children have an abrupt or prolonged separation from their parent or primary care giver as a child. This abrupt separation can lead to an unhealthy attachment and to future psychopathologies in interpersonal relationships as adults, including separation anxiety. Because of the separation anxiety demonstrated by Shareek and other tutees, I would like to use attachment theory as a framework to be applied in future research studies to understand the tutor-tutee relationship and how this relationship impacts the tutee's learning process.

Teacher Perceptions

In my study, teachers' voices were absent. You do not hear those teachers whom participants claimed were racist and homophobic, yelled, put students in closets, and committed other acts that could contribute to inadequate education. Conversely, participants stated that some teachers did actually care for them. They stated that those teachers were caring because they explained homework assignments comprehensively, stayed after school to help with homework assignments, and encouraged students. After reviewing my data, I wondered who these teachers were. What did they believe to be the truth behind the stories of these seven young African American males' perspectives? In other words, what are the teacher perceptions of teacher-student caring relationships?

For instance, Jerele talked at length about Ms. Manbahs and teacher care. He gave a vivid depiction of the way she cared for him, including staying after school and being patient with him. He expressed that Ms. Manbahs had an endless amount of patience when she explained homework assignments. On the other hand, when I reflected on Taylor's disgust of Mr. Ancelman, it was a different story altogether. Taylor reported that Mr. Ancelman did not care for students, did not have challenging assignments, and lacked classroom management. How would Mr. Ancelman interpret these comments? Mr. Ancelman's perspective could have broadened the understanding of this teacher-student relationship. Therefore, in order to obtain a holistic view of a situation, it is imperative that future research investigates the teachers' perspectives as well. This holistic view of the teacher-student relationship can then have a profound impact on interventions designed for lessening inadequate education.

Identity Development

Through further reflection on my data, I began to notice the concept of identity development among my tutees. All of my tutees enjoy the fact that I am an African American male. Even though they may not discuss this openly, all of the parents have expressed their gratitude for my gender and race. Before I met Shane, I had a phone conversation with Mr. Martinson about Shane's academic goals. During our conversation he asked if I was Black. I remember laughing to myself thinking about the directness of this question, but more specifically, I appreciated his respect for his adopted son's race.

My respect and admiration have grown for Mr. Martinson, especially since Shane and I have discussed race in many of our conversations. Shane has also divulged his honesty about the issues of race in his identity development. For example, Shane and I discussed racism frequently in our tutorial sessions. He talked extensively about his experiences with racist teachers at school, but more often about racism in his community. He recently described an incident he and his friend experienced:

> A: And when you say racism, what do you mean by that, can you talk about your definition of racism?
>
> S: Uh, walking like up on Lawrence Street (a street in Jackson, California), walking on Lawrence Street, on, you, you go up in some Asian stores, I remember I went in there with my friends, um, we went in the back of the store, the um Asian guy, he just followed us the whole way, like he didn't, he didn't even keep, he didn't take one eye off us, like he didn't turn around for one thing and then these, these Asian people went in there while we was in there and they was walking, they was all the way in the front, he didn't even go up to them. He was just following us the whole time (Interview with Shane, Wednesday, June 4, 2008).

Shane's experience with racism emphasized a two-fold existence many African Americans experience daily. Although this incident could have been perceived in many ways, Shane was angered because he felt the store employee treated his friend and him differently from other Asian patrons. Regardless, the store employee's discriminatory actions made these young African American males feel devalued. Whereas, the Asian patrons freely shopped devoid of any apparent duality in their sense of self. This incident could have had an enduring and dangerous effect on Shane's identity development. Because of one person's demonstration of bigotry, Shane has to ponder the discrepancy in value as an African American male in two different environments: home and community.

According to Du Bois (1903) post-slavery Blacks often had to reflect about their identity through double-consciousness. This dual reflection process is not only inhumane but immoral. African Americans help built this country and established an enormous amount of wealth for southern White landowners. After slavery, Blacks were forgotten by southern Whites and devalued by most Whites across the United States (Bennett, 2003). It is unfortunate that in the 21st century, many Blacks, including my tutees, have to reflect upon their identity and their value as a human being through this double-consciousness.

Therefore, this notion of identity development should be further researched considering the work of Du Bois (1903) and the experiences of African American males. Future research can explore this identity development process by examining the impact of a relationship with an African American tutor on an African American tutee's identity development. This investigation can also shed some light on the impact of mainstream America on young African American male's identity development. Finally, research on this aspect may reveal information on how young African American males validate their identity throughout their daily experience in mainstream America. I hope all of these components of future research discussed above will ultimately show us ways of reducing inadequate education among African American children.

Recommendations for Practice

The results of this study have revealed the complexity of finding a solution to the inadequate education of African American males. Based on my findings, I believe the most significant areas of future practice involve an African American male forum and daily mentoring.

African American Male Forum

My aspirations for an African American male forum originated from the lack of voice student participants felt in public schools. Many of the student participants and parents described incidents of racism that students experienced in and out of school. When these participants were asked about how they followed-up with these events, many of them pursued the perpetrators, such as talking to their teachers in conferences with parents, while others did nothing. Providing an African American male forum could inspire young Black males to speak out about their culture and the injustices that happen to them in public schools and in their community.

The purpose of an African American male forum is to provide African American males a safe place within the schools for a continuous dialogue to take place. The dialogues could be held on a weekly basis with the intent to discuss young African American males' current struggles in education and to construct solutions through the lens of their African heritage and worldview. These dialogues can be used as a means for African American males to vent, discuss their successes and failures in education, and generate solutions without feeling controlled. The forum could also allow African American males to discuss freely and resolve their own problems as they deem appropriate. In this forum, African American males can voice the pernicious incidences and make connections with their peers who may be facing similar problems of racism, uncaring teachers, culturally irrelevant curriculum, and other inadequacies.

Daily Mentoring

All of my tutees and their parents expressed that students wanted to spend more time with the tutor. The daily mentoring I provide to my tutees has been central to the overall success of my program, particularly the caring relationship which includes critically conscious conversations. As humans I believe we, most of the time, operate on an intellectually superficial level. I find this to be true for many of the adults involved with my tutees. Often these adults associate video games, movies, and amusement parks as relationship. In these environments, adults can opt out of communicating and fostering a meaningful relationship with children. I understand a child needs to play, but I also believe a child needs to connect on a deeper level. This is especially true for young African American males who face many challenges in a hostile society. I find these unconnected relationships inadequate because many of my tutees lack African American male role models with whom they can have a simple conversation.

Given this lack of African American male mentorship, I believe that young African American males need to have a relationship based upon a deep personal connection within their urban school. In this daily mentoring program, adult African American male mentors can shadow young African American males while in school. In the course of shadowing, adult African American males can mentor young African American males about navigating mainstream education, especially institutional problems such as uncaring teachers, excessive detentions, misplacement in special education, and disproportionate suspensions. In the event young African American males encounter these predicaments, adult African American males would be readily available to advocate for them.

Moreover, African American male mentors can take young African American males on walks, engaging them in conversations about being young African American men in urban schools. Mentoring young African American males could help guide them through trials and tribulations they may encounter in mainstream America. In addition, daily mentoring can help them construct a positive sense of self, when the social construction of an African American male is anything but positive.

Conclusion

Young African American males who attend urban schools are continuously being tracked, disproportionally placed in special education, excessively suspended, and experiencing high drop-out rates (California Department of Education, 2005; Kunjufu, 2005; Smiley, 2006). My study suggested how in-home, one-one-one tutoring can buffer these inadequacies. No prior research existed on African American males' perceptions of the tutor-tutee relationship in in-home, one-on-one tutoring. My study narrowed the gap in this research by showing that tutor-tutee caring relationships can have a positive impact on the educational experiences of young African American males. The findings of this study revealed that young African American males became more interested in their academics, acquired life skills, increased reading scores, and successfully navigated the tribulations in their schools because of the care demonstrated by their tutor.

This study could help researchers, parents, and administrators who are concerned in developing enrichment programs for African American males by providing them a model for practice with young African American males. The tutor-tutee caring relationship was the essence of my study in that this relationship embodied Vygotskyan (1978) theory. Student participants in this study stated that the care demonstrated by their tutor was the most common reason why the students had positive experiences with both public school and in-home, one-on-one tutoring.

The findings revealed that tutor-tutee care positively influenced young African American males in in-home, one-on-one tutoring. In particular, student participants and parents highlighted father-like care as central to the success of the tutor-tutee relationship. For this reason, my research is significant and adds to the scholarly research on the impact of care.

APPENDIXES

APPENDIX A

EMAIL APPROVAL OF HUMAN SUBJECTS REQUEST

IRB Application # 08-047 - Application Approved
From:irbphs (irbphs@usfca.edu)
Sent: Fri 5/16/08 3:36 PM
To: ██
Cc: Susan Roberta Katz (katz@usfca.edu)

May 16, 2008

Dear Mr. Horn:

The Institutional Review Board for the Protection of Human Subjects (IRBPHS) at the University of San Francisco (USF) has reviewed your request for human subjects approval regarding your study. Your application has been approved by the committee (IRBPHS #08-047). Please note the following:

1. Approval expires twelve (12) months from the dated noted above. At that time, if you are still in collecting data from human subjects, you must file a renewal application.

2. Any modifications to the research protocol or changes in instrumentation (including wording of items) must be communicated to the IRBPHS. Re-submission of an application may be required at that time.

3. Any adverse reactions or complications on the part of participants must be reported (in writing) to the IRBPHS within ten (10) working days.

If you have any questions, please contact the IRBPHS at (415) 422-6091. On behalf of the IRBPHS committee, I wish you much success in your research.

Sincerely,
Terence Patterson, EdD, ABPP
Chair, Institutional Review Board for the Protection of Human Subjects

APPENDIX B

PARTICIPANT/STUDENT CONSENT FORM

UNIVERSITY OF SAN FRANCISCO

CONSENT FOR STUDENT TO PARTICIPATE IN RESEARCH

Purpose and Background

Mr. Aaron Horn, a doctoral student in the School of Education at the University of San Francisco, is doing a study on the values of caring relationships within in-home, one-on-one tutoring. He is interested in learning about African American males' perceptions on the importance of a caring relationship between tutor and tutee within in-home, one-on-one tutoring. My child is being asked to participate because he has a perception of in-home, one-on-one tutoring.

Procedures

If I agree to allow my child to be in this study, the following will happen:

1. My child will be interviewed one time individually for thirty minutes with open-ended questions.

2. The researcher will transcribe my son's interview and have him verify for authenticity.

Risks and/or Discomforts

1. My child may become uncomfortable or upset during the 30-minute individual interview. If this happens, the researcher will attempt to comfort my son. If my son continues to be upset, the researcher will help facilitate his leaving. My son is free to decline any questions and he can stop participation at any time.

2. Participation in research may mean a loss of confidentiality. Study records will be kept as confidential as is possible. No individual identities will be used in any reports or publications resulting from the study. Study information will be coded and kept in locked files at all times. Only study personnel will have access to the files.

Benefits
There will be no direct benefit to me or to my child from participating in this study. The anticipated benefit of this study is a better understanding of tutor-tutee caring relationships.

Costs/Financial Considerations
There will be no cost to me or to my child as a result of taking part in this study.

Payment/Reimbursement
Neither my child nor I will be reimbursed for participation in this study.

Questions
I have talked to Mr. Aaron Horn about this study and have had my questions answered. If I have further questions about the study, I may call him at ▌▌▌▌▌▌ or Dr. Susan Katz at (415) 422-2209. If I have any questions or comments about participation in this study, I should first talk with the researcher. If for some reason I do not wish to do this, I may contact the IRBPHS, which is concerned with protection of volunteers in research projects. I may reach the IRBPHS office by calling (415) 422-6091 and leaving a voicemail message, by FAX at (415) 422-5528, by e-mailing IRBPHS@usfca.edu, or by writing to the:

Institutional Review Board for the Protection of Human Subjects
University of San Francisco, School of Education
School of Education, Room 023
Department of Counseling Psychology
2130 Fulton Street
San Francisco, California 94117-1080

Consent
I have been given a copy of the "Research Subject's Bill of Rights," and I have been given a copy of this consent form to keep. PARTICIPATION IN RESEARCH IS VOLUNTARY. I am free to decline to have my child be in this study, or to withdraw my child from it at any point. My decision as to whether or not to have my child participate in this study will have no influence on my child's present or future status as a patient in my pediatrician's office. My signature below indicates that I agree to allow my child to participate in this study.

_____   _____
Signature of Subject's Parent/Guardian   Date of Signature

_____   _____
Signature of Person Obtaining Consent   Date of Signature

APPENDIX C

RESEARCH SUBJECTS' BILL OF RIGHTS

The rights below are the rights of every person who is asked to be in a research study. As a participant, I have the following rights:

1. To be told what the study is trying to find out;

2. To be told what will happen to me and whether any of the procedures, drugs, or devices are different from what would be used in standard practice;

3. To be told about the frequent and/or important risks, side effects, or discomforts of the things that will happen to me for research purposes;

4. To be told if I can expect any benefit from participating, and, if so, what the benefit might be;

5. To be told of the other choices I have and how they may be better or worse than being in the study;

6. To be allowed to ask any questions concerning the study, both before agreeing to be involved and during the course of the study;

7. To be told what sort of medical or psychological treatment is available if any complications arise;

8. To refuse to participate at all or change my mind about participation after the study is started; if I were to make such a decision, it will not affect my right to receive the care or privileges I would receive if I were not in the study;

9. To receive a copy of the signed and dated consent form; and

10. To be free of pressure when considering whether I wish to agree to be in the study.

APPENDIX D

RIGHT TO CONFIDENTIALITY/PSEUDONYM ASSIGNMENT

As a participant for this study, please indicate your feelings regarding confidentiality.

CHECK ONE OF THE FOLLOWING:

_____ Please use my legal name in all documentation required to complete the above-mentioned research study.

OR

_____ Please conceal my identity by using a pseudonym in referring to me in the documentation required to complete the above-mentioned research study.

CHECK ONE OF THE FOLLOWING:

_____ Please use the pseudonym _____ when referring to me in the documentation required to complete the above-mentioned research study.

OR

_____ Please choose a pseudonym for me.

PLEASE READ, SIGN, AND DATE:

I understand that I have the right to speak candidly yet confidentially for this research study. By checking the above sections, I am either granting permission to use my legal name or asking to be referred to by a pseudonym.

_____   _____
Signature   Date

APPENDIX E

Data Analysis Tables

Table 4

Color Coded Research Themes (Limitations observed in Teaching and Tutoring)

Theme	Participant/ Caregiver
KT (Kids made fun of his liver transplant scars	Jerele, Jerele's Mother
KT (Kids made fun of his partial amputee fingers)	Dario, Dario's Mother, Dario's Grandmother
PT (Teachers give up on students)	Shane's Father, Taylor's Uncle
PT (Teacher yell at students)	Dario, Dario's Mom, Jerele, Shareek, Shareek's Mother
PT (Teachers don't care)	Dario's Mother, Jerele, Jeremiah, Shane's Father, Shareek, Shareek's Mother, Taylor's Uncle
PT (Teachers issue excessive suspensions and detentions)	Dario, Jeremiah, Jeremiah's Mother, Shareek, Shareek's Mother, Taylor
PT (Teacher failed to establish connection)	Shane's Father, Shareek
PT (Teachers are racist)	Jamie, Jamie's Grandmother, Jeremiah, Jeremiah's Mother, Shane, Shareek, Shareek's Mother, Taylor

Note. KT = Kids Teasing (Orange), PT = Poor Teaching (Red)

122

Table 5
Color Coded Research Themes (Strengths Observed in Teaching and Tutoring)

Theme	Participant/ Caregiver
ES (Learned something new)	Dario, Shareek
ET (Students/ Caregiver appreciates tutor)	Dario's mother, Dario's Grandmother, Jerele, Jamie's Mother, Jeremiah's Mother, Shareek's Mother, Taylor
ET (Students enjoy being around tutor)	Dario, Dario's Mother, Shareek, Shareek's Mother, Taylor's Uncle
ET (Students want more tutoring)	Dario, Dario's Mother,Taylor
GTCH (Teachers helped them with homework)	Dario, Jamie, Jerele
GTCH (Teachers encouraged them)	Dario, Jamie, Jerele, Shane, Shane's Father
GTCH (Teachers established connection)	Shane's Father, Shareek
GTTR (Tutor exposed them to college)	Jerele's Mother, Jeremiah, Taylor
GTTR (Tutor encouraged them)	Dario, Dario's Grandmother, Jerele's Mother, Jeremiah, Shane, Shane's Father, Shareek, Taylor

Note. ES = Enjoys School (Blue), GTCH = Good Teaching (Sky Blue), KAIS = Knowledge Acquired in School (Lime), ET = Enjoys Tutoring (Bright Green), GTTR = Good Tutoring (Dark Teal), KAIT = Knowledge Acquired in Tutoring (Plum), PGCBT = Personal Growth Caused By Tutoring (Lavender), PIHT = Prefers In-Home Tutoring (Blue-Gray), PTAT = Prefers Teaching and Tutoring (Sea Green).

Table 6

Color Coded Research Themes (Strengths Observed in Teaching and Tutoring)

Theme	Participant/ Caregiver
GTTR (Tutor exposed them to library/ bookstore)	Jeremiah, Jeremiah's Mother, Taylor
KAIT (Learned how to organize schoolwork)	Jerele, Jerele's Mother
KAIT (Improved Reading skills)	Dario, Dario's Grandmother, Jamie, Jerele's Mother Shareek, Shareek's Mother, Taylor, Taylor's Uncle
KAIT (Improved Math skills)	Dario's Grandmother, Jamie's Mother, Jerele's Mother, Jeremiah's Mother, Shane, Shane's Father
KAIT (Learned about Black History)	Dario, Jamie, Jerele, Jeremiah, Shane, Taylor, Jeremiah, Shane,
PGCBT (Trust in Black men)	Dario's Mother
PGCBT (Pays attention more)	Shane, Jerele's Mother

Note. ES = Enjoys School (Blue), GTCH = Good Teaching (Sky Blue), KAIS = Knowledge Acquired in School (Lime), ET = Enjoys Tutoring (Bright Green), GTTR = Good Tutoring (Dark Teal), KAIT = Knowledge Acquired in Tutoring (Plum), PGCBT = Personal Growth Caused By Tutoring (Lavender), PIHT = Prefers In-Home Tutoring (Blue-Gray), PTAT = Prefers Teaching and Tutoring (Sea Green)

APPENDIX F

Table 7
Sample Ebonics Phrases Spoken by Research Participants from Delores Heights.

PHRASE	MEANING
Block	The street in which you live and represent
Bounce	To leave, go away, expeditiously
Crackin'	A very exciting environment. To be excited or engaged
Do your thizal!	To take care of personal business; to proud of someone
Fa sho	To be surprised or amazed!
Get wit dem (syn. Scrap)	To fight or interact with a group of people immediately
Hecka	A large amount of something
Holla at cha boy	To inquire about someone's feeling; communicate later
Hommies (syn. Potnas)	Friends from the community.
I got cho back	To take care of someone with complete commitment
Keep it on da real	Being truthful
Off da chain	Referring to someone or something as good or bad
Peeps (syn. ya' boy, pimpin')	Ascribing legitimacy to someone close
Po po (syn. Elroy)	Police
Scrilla (syn. papes, cheese)	Vocabulary for money
What chu finna get into	Inquiring about future activities
What it do?	Inquiring about someone's life.

REFERENCES

Anderson, J. (1988). *The education of Blacks in the South, 1860-1935*. Chapel Hill and London: University of North Carolina Press.

Bennett, L. (2003). *Before the Mayflower: A history of Black America (6th ed)*. Chicago: Penguin Books.

Beyth-Marom, R., Yafe, E., Privman, M., & Harpaz, H.R. (2001). *Satellite home tutorials vs. satellite classroom tutorials* (ED 466 136). Study presented at a world conference on education multimedia, hypermedia, and telecommunications, Tampere, Finland. Retrieved February 27, 2007, from ERIC.

Bondy, E., & Davis, S. (2000, Summer). The caring of strangers: Insights from a field experience in a culturally unfamiliar community. *Action in Teacher Education, 22*, 54-66. Retrieved November 4, 2005, from ERIC.

Bowlby, J. (1969). *Attachment and loss, Vol. 1: Attachment*. New York: Basic Books.

Brown v. Board of Education, 347 U.S. 483 (1954). Retrieved September 18, 2008, from LEXISNEXIS.

California Department of Education. (2005). *High school drop out rates*. Retrieved February 26, 2008 from CDE.CA.GOV.

Caserta-Henry, C. (1996). Reading buddies: A first-grade intervention program. *TheReading Teacher, 49*, 500-503. Retrieved August 7, 2007, from ERIC.

Coleman, J. S. (1990). *Foundations of social theory*. Cambridge: Harvard University Press.

Cooper, R., & Jordan, W. J. (2002, December). *Cultural issues related to high school reform: Deciphering the case of black males* (CRESPAR-R-60). Version of a report presented at a symposium on African American male achievement, Washington, DC. Retrieved December 1, 2005, from ERIC.

Creswell, J. (2003). *Research design: Qualitative, quantitative, and mixed methods approaches* (2nd ed.). Thousand Oaks, CA: Sage Publications.

Dance, J. L. (2002). *Tough fronts: The impact of street culture on schooling.* New York, NY: Routledge.

Du Bois, W.E.B. (1903). *The souls of Black folk. Essays and sketches.* Chicago: A.C.

Ester, T., & Harrison, M. (2004, September). *Pollution, health, environmental racism, and injustice: A toxic inventory of Bayview Hunters Point, San Francisco.* Report presented by the Bayiew Hunter's Point Mothers Environmental Health and Justice Committee Huntersview Tenants Association Greenaction for Health and Environmental Justice, San Francisco, CA. Retrieved July 9, 2007 from ERIC.

Fashola, O. (2005). *Educating African American males: Voices from the field.* Thousand Oaks, CA: Corwin Press.

Fine, L. (2002). Disparate measures. *Education Week, 21,* 34-36. Retrieved September 10, 2008, from PROQUEST.

Fine, M., Weis, L., Weseen, S., & Wong, L. (2006). For whom? Qualitative research, representations, and social responsibilities. In M. Denzin & Y. Lincoln (Eds.), *The landscape of qualitative research. Theories and issues* (2nd ed.). (pp. 107-131). Thousand Oaks, CA: Sage Publications.

Freire, P. (1992). *Pedagogy of the oppressed.* New York, NY: Continuum.

Freire, P. (2005). *Education for critical consciousness.* (2nd Ed). New York, NY: Continuum.

Gay, G. (2005). Education equality for students of color. In J. Banks, & C. Banks (Eds.), *Multicultural education: Issues and perspective* (5th ed.) (pp. 211-241). Hoboken, NJ: John Wiley & Sons, Inc.

Gordon, E. (2006). Establishing a system of public education in which all children achieve at high levels and reach their full potential. In T. Smiley (Ed.), *The covenant with Black America* (pp. 23-45). Chicago, IL: The World Press.

Hock, M., Pulvers, K., & Deshler, D. (2001). The effects of an after-school tutoring program on the academic performance of at-risk students and students with learning disabilities. *Journal of Remedial and Special Education*, 22, 172-186. Retrieved July 28, 2007, from ERIC.

Hook, C., & DuPaul, G. (1999). Parent tutoring for students with attention-deficit/ hyperactivity disorder: Effects on reading performance at school and home. *School Psychology Review*, 28, 60-75. Retrieved August 11, 2007, from ERIC.

Katz, S.R. (1999). Teaching in tensions: Latino immigrant youth, their teachers, and the structures of schooling. *Teachers College Record, 100(4)*, 809-840.

Kunjufu, J. (2002). *Black students, middle-class teachers.* Chicago: African American Images.

Kunjufu, J. (2005). *Keeping Black boys out of special education.* Chicago: African American Images.

Ladson-Billings, G. (1994). *The dreamkeepers: Successful teachers of African American children.* San Francisco: Jossey-Bass Publishers.Ladson-Billings, G. (2000). Racialized discourses and ethnic epistemologies. In N. Denzin & Y. Lincoln (Eds.), *Handbook of qualitative research* (2nd ed.) (pp. 107-131). Thousand Oaks, CA: Sage Press.

Ladson-Billings, G., & Tate, W. F. (1995). Toward a critical race theory of education. *Teachers College Record, 97(1)*, 47-69.

Madden, N. A., & Slavin, R. E. (2001, April). *Reducing the gap: Success for all and the achievement of African American and Latino students.* (ED455079). Paper presented at the annual meeting of the American Educational Research Association, Seattle, WA. Retrieved November 23, 2005, from ERIC.

Martin, W. E. (1998). *What Brown v. Board of Education should have said: A brief history with documents.* New York: Bedford/ St. Martin's.

Noddings, N. (1992). *The challenge to care in schools: An alternative approach to education.* New York, NY: Teachers College Press.

Noguera, P. (2003). *City schools and the American dream: Reclaiming the promise of public school education.* New York: Teachers College Press.

Noguera, P. (2005). The trouble with Black boys: The role and influence of environmental and cultural factors on the academic performance of African American males. In O. Fashola, *Educating African American males: Voices from the field* (pp. 51-79). Thousand Oaks, CA: Corwin Press.

Plessy v. Ferguson, 163 U.S. 537 (1896). Retrieved November 11, 2007, from LEXISNEXIS.

Schott Foundation for Public Education. (2006). Public *education and black male students* . Retrieved February15, 2008, from SCHOTTFOUNDATION.ORG.

Smiley, T. (2006). *The covenant with Black America.* Chicago: Third World Press.

Stanton-Salazar, R. (1997). A social capital framework for understanding the socialization of racial minority children and youths. *Harvard Educational Review 67*, 1-40.

Valenzuela, A. (1999). *Subtractive schooling. U.S.-Mexican youth and the politics of caring.* New York: State University of New York.

Vygotsky, L. S. (1978). Interaction between learning and development. In M. Cole, V. John-Steiner, ˙S. Scribner, & E. Souberman (Eds.), *Mind in society: The development of higher psychological processes* (pp. 84-91). Cambridge, MA: Harvard University Press.

Yogev, A., & Ronen, R. (1982). Cross-age tutoring: Effects on tutors' attributes. *Journal of Educational Research, 75*, 261-268. Retrieved July 28, 2007, from ERIC.

INDEX

132

Z

Aaron L. Horn

Dr. Aaron L. Horn is an Educational Consultant for the non-profit agency Brainstorm Tutoring in San Francisco, California. Dr. Horn received his Ed.D. in International Multicultural Education from the University of San Francisco.